SIX THINKING HATS FOR SCHOOLS

3-5 Resource Book

by
Edward de Bono

This series of teacher resource books represents the only authorized
educational adaptation of the six hats method. This material
is written and designed by the originator of the six hats
method, Edward de Bono, specifically for use in education.

Consultants:

Tonda L. Daugherty
Fifth and Sixth Grade Teacher
Conn-West Elementary School
Kansas City, Missouri

Reva Hairston
Principal
Terrell Elementary School
Chicago, Illinois

Linda H. Drollinger
Third Grade Teacher
Chouteau Elementary School
Kansas City, Missouri

Sandy O'Brien
Fifth Grade Teacher
Maplewood Elementary School
Kansas City, Missouri

Catherine C. Hatala
Humanities Coordinator
School District of Philadelphia
Philadelphia, Pennsylvania

Phyllis S. Renshaw
Fourth Grade Teacher
Southeast Elementary Park Hill
Kansas City, Missouri

Editor-in-Chief: Kathleen Myers
Managing Editor: Beth Obermiller
Editors: Mary Lindeen
Rebecca Schwartz
Sue Thies
Cover and Book Design: Barbara Gordon
Photography: Craig Anderson

ISBN 1-56312-097-6

Published by Perfection Learning Corporation
Copyright 1991. The McQuaig Group Inc.

"If we put the factory at that place, then if there is an accident, toxic chemicals will flow into the town's water supply."

"If you go to work in the kitchen with that thumb infection, you could make a lot of people ill with food poisoning."

"If you drop out of school, you will find it harder to get a job for the rest of your life."

We need to be careful to avoid doing things that might do harm to the environment, to others, or to ourselves. What sort of thinking protects us from making such mistakes? This is black hat thinking.

Obviously, black hat thinking is a very important part of thinking. In fact, you could say that black hat thinking may be the most important type of thinking. Certainly the black hat is the most used hat.

I make this point because some people have got the idea that somehow the black hat is not as useful as the other hats. This is an incorrect view based on two mistakes.

1. Because black hat thinking is often used to point out bad things does not mean it is bad thinking.

2. Because overuse and abuse of the black hat may limit thinking does not mean that the black hat as such is a bad hat. Eating too much may make you ill, but this does not mean that food is bad. Drinking too much alcohol may make you an alcoholic, but this does not mean that beer and wine are themselves bad.

This is an important point because all six thinking hats are valuable types of thinking. To consider any one hat as inferior to the others destroys the usefulness of the system.

Without the black hat, we would get into a lot of trouble and cause a lot of harm.

TABLE OF CONTENTS

. . . simple methods used effectively are more valuable than complicated methods that are difficult to understand

Edward de Bono is a pioneer in the field of the teaching of thinking in education. He first wrote the CoRT program in 1972. This program is now the most widely used program throughout the world for the direct teaching of thinking as a curriculum subject. It is used in the USA, China, USSR, Venezuela, United Kingdom, Nepal, Malaysia, Australia, New Zealand, and in many other countries. This widespread use of Dr. de Bono's material across different nationalities and cultures is due to the simplicity and robustness of the material. The material can be used by teachers with widely differing backgrounds and qualifications.

Dr. de Bono was a Rhodes scholar at Oxford University and has held faculty appointments at the universities of Oxford, Cambridge, London, and Harvard. He has written thirty books in the general area of thinking. There are translations into twenty-three languages including Japanese, Hebrew, Finnish, Russian, and Urdu.

What is unusual about Dr. de Bono is that he works in the field of education and also for business and government organizations. He has worked with such corporations as IBM, DuPont, Hoechst-Celanese, and many others.

The Six Thinking Hats method is based on Dr. de Bono's very extensive experience in the field of the direct teaching of thinking across different ages and abilities, ranging from six-year-olds to senior corporate executives. It is Dr. de Bono's belief that simple methods used effectively are more valuable than complicated methods that are difficult to understand and confusing to use.

This book is one of a series of resource books for the teaching of the six thinking hats method in schools. The series includes a book for each of these levels: grades K-2, 3-5, 6-8, 9-12, and adults. The use of the method is valid at all ages. The teaching of the method will, however, vary with age and ability.

With younger students, the use of each hat can be simplified. With older and more able students, the use of each hat is more comprehensive and more precise. Simpler exercises are chosen for younger students. There are more difficult exercises provided in the upper-level books.

Time and Place

In some schools, there is a specific allocation of time to the direct teaching of thinking skills. In such cases, the six hats method can be taught directly as part of the thinking skills program.

In schools where there is as yet no provision for the direct teaching of thinking skills, the six hats method can be taught as part of other subject areas. For example, there is always a close link between language and thinking. Language is there to express thinking. If the thinking is poor, then language skills by themselves will not be much use. So the six hats method could be taught as part of language arts.

The six hats framework is also valuable for writing about or discussing any subject. Therefore, the method may be taught as part of such subject areas as reading, social studies, science, or math.

My experience suggests that thinking skills are most effectively taught if they are taught directly and deliberately. So I recommend the direct teaching of the six hats method—with subsequent infusion into other areas. Where this is not practical, then the method can be taught as part of some existing curriculum area—like language.

USING THIS BOOK

. . . thinking skills are most effectively taught if they are taught directly and deliberately

hen we attempt practical thinking, there are three fundamental difficulties:

1. *Emotions.* We often have a tendency not to think at all but to rely on instant gut feeling, emotion, and prejudice as a basis for action.

2. *Helplessness.* We may react with feelings of inadequacy: "I don't know how to think about this. I don't know what to do next."

3. *Confusion.* We try to keep everything in mind at once, with a mess as a result.

The six thinking hats method is a simple and practical way of overcoming all three difficulties.

Emotions are an important part of thinking and, in the end, all decisions and choices are made on the basis of our feelings. Emotions at the right place in thinking are essential. Emotions at the wrong place can be disastrous. The six hats method allows us to use emotions and feelings at the right place.

Helplessness arises when we do not have any general-purpose thinking actions that can be taken. The six hats method provides us with a basic framework for thinking actions. There are now definite "next steps" that can be taken.

Confusion arises when we try to do too much at once. Often when we try to think about something, our minds go off in several different directions at the same time. The six hats method allows us to take one direction at a time.

Full-Color Thinking, One Color at a Time

In the kitchen, have you ever found yourself stirring a sauce, chopping up carrots, mixing a batter, and reading a recipe all at the same time?

In the classroom, have you ever found yourself taking attendance, collecting lunch money, making announcements, and tending an ill child all at the same time?

We frequently do this sort of thing with our thinking too. We have to keep the information in mind while also trying to be logical and to make sure others are logical. Our emotions are there all the time too. And we need to be constructive. Occasionally, we might even try to be creative and to produce a new idea. As a result, there is a lot going on all at once.

In full-color printing, the basic colors are printed separately. But in the end, all the colors add up to give full-color printing.

In projection television, we can see that there are three beams, each of which is projecting a different base color. These three colors come together on the screen to give full-color television.

The six hats method does exactly the same for thinking. Instead of trying to do everything at once, we can learn to handle the different aspects of thinking one at a time. In the end, these different aspects come together to give full-color thinking.

Six Colors, Six Hats

In the six hats method, thinking is divided into six different modes, each of which is represented by a different color hat. A brief description of each mode is given here. A full description for each will be provided later.

 Red Hat. Emotions. Intuition, feelings, and hunches. No need to justify the feelings. How do I feel about this right now?

 Yellow Hat. Benefits. Why is this worth doing? What are the benefits? Why can it be done? Why will it work?

 Black Hat. * Caution. Judgment. Assessment. Is this true? Will it work? What are the weaknesses? What is wrong with it?

 Green Hat. Creativity. Different ideas. New ideas. Suggestions and proposals. What are some possible solutions and courses of action? What are the alternatives?

* See the note on page 30 concerning the black hat.

White Hat. Information. Questions. What information do we have? What information do we need to get?

 Blue Hat. Organization of thinking. Thinking about thinking. How far have we come? What step do we take next?

It is possible to suggest many further hats for different aspects of thinking. However, I believe that the six hats are enough. More hats would be cumbersome and confusing. Fewer would be inadequate.

Hats and Role-Playing

Why hats? There is a traditional association between thinking and hats.

"Put on your thinking cap."

"Let's put on our thinking hats here."

A hat is very simple to put on and to take off. No other piece of clothing can be put on or taken off so quickly and easily. This is relevant because we must be able to put on or take off the different colored hats with ease.

Also, hats often indicate a role. Soldiers can wear special helmets. The police may wear hats to indicate their role. In some countries, judges wear special hats. So as we put on a thinking hat, we take on the role indicated by that particular hat.

Switching Roles

It is very important that every thinker must be able to switch roles: put hats on, take hats off. The hats are not meant to put people into categories. It is totally wrong to say "She's a green hat thinker" or "He only uses the red hat." Although these may be accurate assessments, if we start to use the hats as categories, then people only want to use the thinking associated with a particular category: "I am a black hat thinker." This is exactly the opposite of the purpose and value of the six hats method, which is to get people to use all six modes of thinking.

Detaching the Ego

One of the great limiting factors in thinking is that our egos are much too involved in our thinking. Our egos get attached to an idea or an argument. We cannot stand back in order to be objective. The role-playing of the six hats method allows the ego to be detached from the thinking.

"This is not me but my black hat (yellow, green, etc.) speaking."

It is in this way that the six hats method takes the ego out of thinking.

Getting Beyond Argument

Normally, if we think an idea is not workable, we will spend all our time arguing against it. With the six hats method, we can learn to put on the yellow hat. In doing so, we now show that, even though the idea seems useless, some good may be found in it.

Instead of saying, "This is what I think and I know I am right," we can learn to say, "If you want me to play the yellow hat role, I can do that very well."

We develop a pride in the skill of carrying out the different thinking roles. As a result, our thinking about any matter is more comprehensive and more objective.

With the six hats method, if we do not like a suggestion, we know that there will always be a chance to criticize that idea with the black hat and to express feeling with the red hat. Meanwhile, it is possible to explore the idea with white, yellow, and green hats as well.

Four Uses of the Hats in the Classroom

1. **Put the hat on.** We can ask a student in a discussion to put on a particular color hat. Or we can ask a whole group to use a particular color hat for a few minutes.

    "I want you to give me some black hat thinking on this idea. What could go wrong if we try this idea out?"

    "We're stuck. Can you put on your green hat and give us some new ideas about this problem?"

    "What are the facts about this? What do we know about this? Give us your white hat thinking."

2. **Take the hat off.** We can ask someone, or a group, to take off a particular color of hat. Here we are implying that the thinking that is taking place is of a certain type. We are asking the student to move away from that type of thinking. The six hats system provides a convenient method for this. The student has not consciously put on a hat but seems to be using one.

    "That's red hat thinking. Can you take off your red hat for a moment?"

    "You have given us good black hat thinking. Now please take off your black hat."

    "You've thought of lots of new ideas and possibilities, but I think we should take off our green hats now."

3. **Switch hats.** Once the rules have been established, we can ask for an instant switch in thinking. We can accomplish this by suggesting that a student take off one hat and put on another. This way we can call for a switch in thinking without offending the student. We

are not attacking the thinking that is taking place but asking for a change.

> "We've heard the good things. Now let's switch from the yellow hat to the black hat. Where might we run into trouble if we do it this way?"

> "With your black hat, you've done a good job of telling why this idea might not work. Now let's switch to the green hat to see if we can fix these problems."

> "That's an interesting idea. Now let's take off our green hats and put on our white hats. For now, let's talk only about the facts."

4. **Signal your thinking.** We can name a hat to show the type of thinking that we are going to use. For instance, sometimes something needs to be said but is difficult to say without giving offense. Putting on the black hat makes it possible to discuss an idea without attacking the person who offered it. Use the hats yourself—and point out that you are using them—as you teach the hats to the class.

> "Putting on my black hat, I'm thinking that it won't work to get out the musical instruments now because we won't have enough time to put them away before lunch."

> "Putting on my red hat for a moment, I have to say that I just do not like the idea of using those shelves for the science books. I'm not sure why."

> "Putting on my green hat, I want to tell you a new idea I thought of for those of you who are working on the computer today. It is only a suggestion."

In summary, we can ask students to put on, take off, switch or signal hats. We can also put on or take off a hat ourselves. The formality and "game" aspect of the method is one of its greatest virtues. People learn to play the game.

Single Hat and Sequence Use

The hats can be used singly at any point in thinking. In general, this is the major use. The hats are used as a convenience for directing thinking and for switching thinking.

Simple sequences of two or three hats may be used together for a particular purpose. For example, the yellow hat followed by the black hat may be used to assess an idea. The black hat followed by the green hat may be used to improve a design (point out the faults and overcome them).

A full sequence of hats may be used as a framework for thinking about a subject. This framework is set up in advance as a program for thinking—a thinking agenda. The thinkers then follow the steps of that program.

The Unique Blue Hat

The blue hat is different from the other hats because it is involved with directing the thinking process itself. We are actually using the blue hat whenever we suggest the next hat to be used. The blue hat need not be acknowledged at every turn. It can become awkward to say, for instance, "Putting on my blue hat, I feel we should have some black hat thinking."

However, there are some points at which it is often helpful to mention the blue hat. Three such points are at the outset of a discussion, to describe a thinking plan; at midpoint, to restate the thinking goals; and at the end, to summarize what thinking has been done.

"Putting on our blue hats, let's decide what we want to think about and which hats we'll need to use."

"This is interesting but I think we are drifting away from our goal. Who can wear the blue hat and recall our purpose?"

"I want to put on my blue hat here and ask if we can come to a conclusion."

Use of the blue hat need not be confined to talking about the other hats. Any thinking steps at all can be suggested.

Six Hats for Richer Thinking

The six hats method allows students to think more richly and more comprehensively. If we simply ask students to think about something, they are often at a loss. But if they are invited to explore the subject using the framework of the hats, their perceptual powers are quickly expanded. For example, compare the responses given to the following assignment.

Read the poem and tell what you think about it.

> The icy air stings,
> warning an innocent world.
> Watch—winter wants you!
>
> —Anonymous

Unassisted
response: "I really like that poem."

"I think it's a very good poem."

Six Hats
response: **Red hat (feelings)**

"I really like that poem."

"It gives me a feeling of danger."

"I think the poet felt alarmed about the cold—winter can be deadly."

White hat (facts)

"The poem has no title."

"We don't know who wrote it."

"It doesn't rhyme."

"It has three lines."

"The middle line is longest."

"It's about winter coming."

"The world is called 'innocent.' "

Yellow hat (good points)

"Winter sounds like an enemy, sneaking up."

"I can feel the sting of the air. Winter air is like that."

"The last line has a lot of *w* sounds: 'watch,' 'winter,' 'wants.' They make a whispering sound."

" 'Watch—winter wants you!' makes me shiver, just like winter does."

(Discussion could be continued with the black and green hats.)

The elaboration in the second example shows how the six hats method can expand students' perception. The hats supply cues but allow for open-ended responses. With the hats, students are able to become more self-directed but without aimless drifting. In the next section, I will begin to talk specifically about teaching and using the six hats.

TEACHING THE HATS

The learning and practicing must be enjoyable.

Sessions introducing the hats should move briskly and discussion should be as practical as possible. As each hat is taught, give repeated clear examples of its uses.

Matters will arise which can be confusing. For example, many ideas may fit under two hats at the same time. There needn't be any problem with this—just identify how you are deciding to accept and make use of the comment.

Student: That's not green hat, that's yellow!

Teacher: Perhaps it's both, because it's stating something good about the situation but also offers a new suggestion. Let's include it on our list under the green hat because we're trying to think of new ideas at the moment.

If the comment is clearly off target, settle the matter quickly and move on.

Student: I think that's a good plan.

Teacher: Your comment is okay for red hat thinking, but we're using the yellow hat right now. What are the good points about the plan? *Why* do you think it's good?

Steps in the Lessons

The actual steps provided in this book for teaching the hats are as follows:

1. **Lead-in.** Begin with a simple illustration, example, or exercise that shows in action the process that is to be taught.

2. **Explanation.** Move at once to explaining what is to be taught—the nature of the selected hat. With eight- to ten-year-olds, this explanation can be rather brief.

3. **Demonstration.** Give more examples demonstrating the process in use. Invite discussion, suggestions, questions, etc.

4. **Practice.** This is the most important part of the teaching. The students themselves use the process on practice items. Offer as many practice items as possible. Do not spend a long time on any one item, as this distracts attention from the process. Remember that the purpose is to teach a skill, not to have an interesting discussion. If one item does not work well, move right on to another item.

5. **Elaboration.** In practicing the process, you and your students may be able to make additional observations on how the process is used. These may arise from the way a particular practice item has been tackled or in answer to questions the students ask. After students have been introduced to each hat, invite them to be alert to times when they are able to use the hat in real life. These observations can be noted in a journal and shared in subsequent class discussions.

6. **Conclusion.** Summarize the process, repeat the main points, and emphasize why the process can be useful.

The Nature of the Practice Items

Many practice items are given in this book. You are free to modify the items and to add your own. Some of the items are fun. Some of the items are remote in the sense that the matter is not of direct concern to students. Other items are local or ''backyard'' items that are of direct concern.

A common mistake in the teaching of thinking skills is to make all practice items relate to issues of great importance. The opposite mistake is to use only puzzles and abstract simulations and to hope that skills learned in such matters will generalize to real-life situations.

Instead, there should be a mix of practice items. Fun and remote items provide better practice of the thinking skill because there is less interference from experience and emotions. Local items are more motivating and are essential from time to time to show that the hats framework can be used for real life, important matters.

Output

The output for the practice items is often verbal, but students can be encouraged to write and even draw pictures to express their thinking. When the output is verbal, a student or a group may wish to read from notes they have taken during their discussions. Where the hats are used in conjunction with language arts or another curriculum subject, the six hat framework can be applied directly to the usual writing activities.

Getting the output from individuals or groups is an important part of practice because it provides the motivation. Anyone who has done any thinking on a subject wants others to hear that thinking.

But keep the feedback crisp and brief so that you can spend more time on actual practice. Don't get involved in arguments on a particular point. If you, as teacher, wish to disagree with a point, then just say that you accept the point but disagree. It is only if the process has been used wrongly that intervention becomes important—in order to prevent the other students from becoming confused.

"We were doing black hat thinking, but your comment is about a new idea we could try. That's the green hat. Let's go back to the black hat for a moment."

In feedback from group work, you may wish to take a point from each group as you go around the class. Or you can ask for a full output from one group and then ask the other groups if they have anything further to add.

Tone

When teaching the six thinking hats, keep the presentation

1. **Focused:** The teaching must be clearly focused on the skill or hat that is being taught. Make a point of repeating the name of the hat as often as possible—even when this seems artificial.

2. **Clear:** Avoid confusion at all costs. If there is confusion, seek to simplify things. Give many clear examples.

3. **Brisk:** The pace must be quick. Keep the practice items short and the feedback fast. Then move on to the next item.

4. **Enjoyable:** The learning and practicing must be enjoyable. This enjoyment arises from the active use of the thinking skill, from lively practice items, and from imaginative answers to stimulate students. If an item does not work well, just drop it and go on to another.

STUDENT OVERVIEW LESSON

In this program, each of the six thinking hats will be examined in detail and taught individually. It is important, however, to give students a broad overview before they explore the hats in depth. Keep this overview very simple; otherwise, students will become confused as they try to remember all six hats.

To begin the overview, give each student a copy of the **Which Hat?** reproducible on page 23. Read the proposal in the box to the students. Then explain that each character in the picture has a different way of thinking about the proposal. Tell the class that you are going to read each character's comment. (Or you may wish to ask six students to read the parts.)

As the parts are read, have students decide which type of thinking each character is doing. Invite them to pick out the appropriate phrase in the box marked "Types of Thinking" and write this phrase in the hat beside the character's name.

After students have had time to complete the reproducible, help them check their worksheets. Discussion notes are provided on page 24.

Which Hat?

Directions: Six different students comment on a proposal. Read the students' comments, then write the type of thinking each is doing in the hat shape next to the person's name.

Proposal: Suppose someone suggests putting salt into ice cream for a new taste.

Types of Thinking		
Look for facts	Find weaknesses	Think about thinking
Tell feelings	Find strengths	Offer new ideas

Jennifer:
I don't like that idea at all!

Carlos:
Maybe they could put salted peanuts in the ice cream.

Aretha:
But it might add a great zingy taste.

Julie:
How much salt would be used?

Max:
It wouldn't work because the salt would melt the ice cream.

Paul:
Why don't we think about the good points first and then the bad points.

Which Hat? · Discussion Notes

If possible, have students outline each hat in color as they correct their work. This will give them a six hats color key to keep for future reference.

Teacher comments for *Jennifer:*
What phrase did you choose to describe Jennifer's thinking? Jennifer tells what she feels about the suggestion. This is red hat thinking. The red hat is for telling what we feel about something. Now outline the hat next to Jennifer's name in red.

Teacher comments for *Aretha:*
Now tell me about Aretha. Aretha finds something good in the idea, a strength. This is yellow hat thinking. With the yellow hat, we look at the good points or benefits. So let's outline Aretha's hat in yellow.

Teacher comments for *Max:*
What about Max? Max tells why the suggestion will not work. Max is finding a weakness in the idea. He is using the black hat. The black hat is for thinking about what is wrong with an idea. Now outline the hat next to Max's name in black.

Teacher comments for *Carlos:*
What phrase did you use to describe Carlos' thinking? Carlos offers a new idea. He has a creative suggestion. This is green hat thinking. Green hat thinking is for possibilities and suggestions. Put a green outline around Carlos' hat.

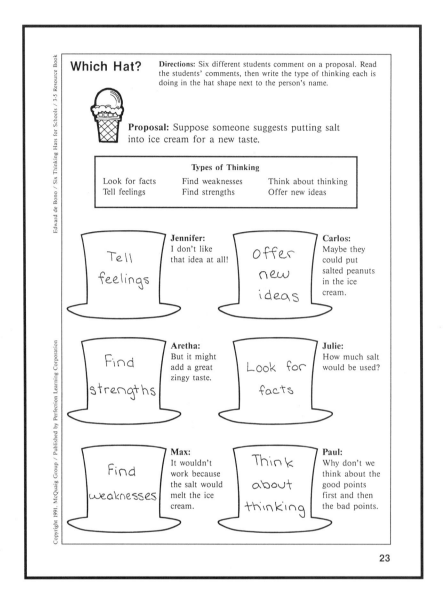

Teacher comments for *Julie:*
How did you describe Julie's thinking? Julie is looking for facts. She asks a question. She wants more information. This is white hat thinking. You can leave Julie's hat white.

Teacher comments for *Paul:*
Finally, we have Paul. What about his thinking? Paul suggests some steps for thinking about the ice cream idea: thinking about thinking. This is blue hat thinking. With the blue hat, we decide what thinking is needed. Make a blue outline around Paul's hat.

Trying On the Hats

After working through the **Which Hat?** overview, explain to the students that they can use these imaginary hats to think better about any subject. Then invite them to try out the hats in thinking about the following proposal. Read the proposal aloud to the students, then help them discuss it, using each hat in turn, as shown below.

> ## Proposal
>
> School should start one hour earlier in the morning and end one hour earlier.

Teacher: Let's have some *red hat thinking*. What are your feelings about that suggestion? Don't explain your reasons; just tell me what you feel. (Pause for replies.)

Sample
responses: I don't like it.
I think it's a dumb idea.
I think it's great.
(If students find it difficult to respond, you can take a poll of their feelings: Raise your hand if you feel it is a good idea. Raise your hand if you feel it is a bad idea. Raise your hand if you feel it is an interesting idea.)

Teacher: Now try the *yellow hat*. Are there any benefits or good points about the idea? Do you have any yellow hat points? (Pause for replies.)

Sample
responses: Ending earlier might be good because you would have more of the day left. Getting to school might be easier because there would be less traffic at that time.

Teacher: Now for some *black hat thinking*. That means looking at what is wrong with the idea, why the idea may not work. Let's have some suggestions. (Pause for replies.)

Sample
responses: People might not want to get up so early in the morning. Students might be more tired during school. Starting to school earlier might require children to walk or travel in the dark, which could be dangerous.

Teacher: What about some creative thinking? What about some new ideas on this, some *green hat thinking*? (Pause.)

Sample
responses: Perhaps students, teachers, and parents could all vote on what time they wanted their school to start. Maybe the earlier starting time could be tried out for one week to see how it works.

Teacher: Now for the *white hat thinking*. What information should we have in order to think about this suggestion? (Pause.)

Sample
responses: We should find out how early the buses start running. We should find out when it gets light at different times in the year.

Teacher: Finally the *blue hat*. What thinking plan have we used to talk about the early-school proposal? Which hat did we wear first? Next? What was the sequence? (Pause.)

Sample
Responses: First, we used the red, to see how we felt about the proposal. Then yellow, to look at the good points. Then black, to find what was wrong with the idea. Then we used the green hat to think of new ideas. And then the white and blue hats.

Note: It is not necessary to come to a final conclusion about the proposal. The purpose of the exercise is to briefly "try on" each thinking hat.

Making Real Hats and Other Visual Aids

Now that students have become acquainted with the hats, you might create and use actual hats. The six hats can be made out of colored paper. Two reproducible hat patterns are provided on pages 164-165. It is also possible to lay circles of colored ribbon on the floor so that someone doing yellow hat thinking, for example, steps into the yellow ring. Or rolled tubes of colored paper can be used by the students to indicate what type of answer is to be given.

Six Thinking Hats Cheer

Children can be taught the following cheer to use as a review. When the cheerleaders say ''red hat,'' the group shouts ''Wow'' (expression of strong feeling). For the yellow hat, the cry is ''Yes'' (the good points). When the leaders say ''black hat,'' the group shouts ''No'' (meaning it is wrong). For the green hat, the cry is ''New'' (for new ideas). For the white hat, the cry is ''Facts'' (for more information). With the blue hat, the group shouts ''Think'' (for choosing how to think about something).

Leader	Group
Red hat	Wow!
Yellow hat	Yes!
Black hat	No!
Green hat	New!
White hat	Facts!
Blue hat	Think!

Call out the different colors in any order. Then let students serve as cheerleaders for subsequent rounds.

Use the six hats cheer as a warm-up before a class begins or whenever you are about to ask the class to use the hats for thinking about a subject. The cheer might be enhanced by displaying cutouts of the hats, real hats, flags, or pompons of each color as the hats are named.

Summary

When the overview session is finished, invite students to help you list what is now known about the six thinking hats. The main points are summarized on the **Six Hats at a Glance** reproducible on page 29.

Subsequent chapters in this book provide suggestions for elaborating on each of the six thinking hats. The suggested activities will help students become more comfortable with the hats and more confident in their use.

If possible, keep the overview session separate and on its own. If, however, time remains which must be used, then go on to the black hat.

Edward de Bono / Six Thinking Hats for Schools / 3-5 Resource Book

Six Hats at a Glance

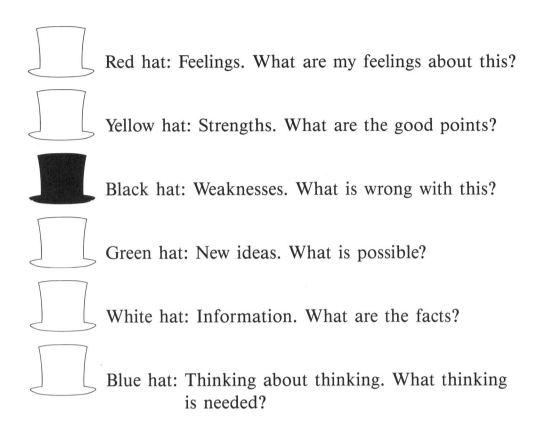

Red hat: Feelings. What are my feelings about this?

Yellow hat: Strengths. What are the good points?

Black hat: Weaknesses. What is wrong with this?

Green hat: New ideas. What is possible?

White hat: Information. What are the facts?

Blue hat: Thinking about thinking. What thinking is needed?

Remember:

✔ There are six different colored hats.

✔ Each hat stands for one kind of thinking.

✔ You can put on or take off one of the hats. When you put on a hat, you play the role attached to that hat.

✔ You can ask someone else to put on a hat, take off a hat, or switch hats.

✔ When you are wearing a hat, you must use only the type of thinking indicated by that hat color.

THE
BLACK
HAT

*What is wrong
with this?*

The black hat is for critical thinking. The word *critical* originally comes from the Greek word for judge (*kritikos*). In many countries, judges in court wear black robes because this is a serious color. You may wish to point out to students that wearing the black hat is a serious job.

It is totally wrong to view black hat thinking as bad or undesirable thinking. Using the black hat protects us from making dangerous or unworkable decisions. With the black hat, we find weaknesses and flaws, and we predict problems that may arise. The black hat is perhaps the most often used and the most valuable of all the hats.

The black hat is discussed in more detail on pages 31-32. Activities for teaching the black hat begin on page 33.

Note: Some teachers who prefer to avoid using the color black have chosen to substitute another color, like gray, for this important thinking process.

TEACHER NOTES · Black Hat

The following description is intended to serve as background for teacher reference. Consult it when needed to clarify how the black hat may be used and overused.

With the black hat, the words *checking* and *checking out* are very important to explaining its uses. These words convey the essence of critical thinking—and do not carry a negative image.

We know the positive uses of checking something:

In the United States when a new drug is presented by a pharmaceutical company, it is thoroughly checked out by the government's Food and Drug Administration to see that it is not harmful.

In the production and serving of food, there are strict rules of hygiene to prevent the people who eat the food from becoming ill. Inspectors are always checking to see that these rules are followed.

When a manufacturer produces a new toy, this has to be thoroughly checked to be sure that it is not harmful—no sharp edges that might cut, no pieces that might be bitten off and swallowed by a child, etc.

The black hat checks things in the same way. Black hat thinking helps us avoid making mistakes and doing silly things. It also points out difficulties and dangers.

Uses of the Black Hat

The main uses of the black hat are these:

1. Checking for evidence
2. Checking for logic
3. Checking for feasibility
4. Checking for impact
5. Checking for fit
6. Checking for weaknesses

We shall examine each of these uses one after the other. As we do, notice that the purpose of the black hat is not to *attack* but to *examine* an idea or situation.

Checking for Evidence

One use of the black hat is to check the evidence which supports the truth of some statement or claim: Is this true? Is this right? Is this correct? What is the evidence that supports this idea?

Checking for Logic

Another use of the black hat is to check the truth or validity of a logical argument: Does this really follow? Someone may claim that if we have *A* and *B*, then *C* must follow. Black hat thinking checks this claim. We might even check the use of the word *must*. It is possible that *C* might follow, but that is not the same as *must* follow. This is a black hat check for logic.

Checking for Feasibility

With the black hat, we may examine a suggestion to see if it is feasible, possible, or likely to work as claimed. Will this invention work? In practice, can this be done? Will this plan succeed?

With questions like these, we may find actual mistakes or gaps or find that something is missing. For example, a faculty committee that is proposing to implement a new kind of student assessment looks to see if its plan is feasible or workable. The black hat asks if this can be done. How will it work? What might be the difficulties?

Checking for Impact

Anything we do has consequences. Our actions affect other people and the world around us. So we need to get input on the impact of the change before making a final decision.

With the black hat, we may check to see what negative effects a suggestion or idea will have. What might be the difficulties? What dangers are likely to arise? How will this affect other people? How will it affect the environment?

The most important part of checking the impact of an idea is the effect it may have on values. Obviously, the idea suits the values of whoever is making the suggestion—but how does the idea affect others' values?

We need to check the impact of a suggestion very carefully. It may be too late to go back after the idea has been put into use.

Checking for Fit

With the black hat, we may check the fit of what is suggested with what we already know. On a very simple level, we might ask, do these clothes fit? Will this fit in the box? Does the plug fit in the socket?

We also may check an idea to see if it fits the facts as we know them. How does this fit our information? Does this idea fit our experience in this field? Does this fit personal or general experience?

We may also want to know whether an item, policy, or plan fits in with a system: Does this fit the rule, the laws, or the regulations? Does this fit the normal procedures? Does this fit our strategies and objectives?

We can check to see if an idea fits our standards and ethics. Does this plan, policy, or item fit the standards and ethics of our group or society—even if this is not a matter of law? Is this fair? Is this honest?

As for values, we could ask, does this fit our values or the values of our group or society? Here we are not talking about what impact the idea will have on values,

TEACHER NOTES · Black Hat

but whether it fits the existing values.

At the end of this assessment, we could say that something fits, does not fit very well, or does not fit at all.

In practice, there is a big difference between looking at an idea in order to attack or reject it and looking at an idea in order to improve it.

Checking for Weaknesses

Suppose we are presented with a design for a new chair. We look for the weaknesses in the design: the seat is too small, the back is too straight, etc. Our intention may be to reject the design because of these weaknesses.

But our intention may also be to improve the design by pointing out the weaknesses so that they can be overcome. This is a constructive function of the black hat. We search for and point out weaknesses in an idea in order to overcome them, thereby making the idea stronger. When the black hat is used this way, it is generally followed by a green hat search for ways to overcome the weaknesses. This sequence is often called *constructive criticism.*

In practice, there is a big difference between looking at an idea

in order to attack or reject it and looking at an idea in order to improve it.

Questions we might ask to check for weaknesses include these: What are the weaknesses here? What are the weak points in the idea? The word *faults* could be used instead of *weaknesses,* but *weakness* seems a more positive word. A weakness may be minor whereas a fault always seems major and perhaps not correctable.

In summary, the uses of the black hat include checking for evidence, logic, feasibility, impact, fit, and weaknesses. Different mental processes go into these various operations. For example, checking for logical truth means applying the rules of logic. Checking for feasibility may mean applying the rules of engineering or experience of human behavior. Checking for impact involves running something forward in our minds and watching the effects.

Purposes for Using the Black Hat

The two main purposes for using the black hat are to

1. Find weaknesses

2. Make assessments

We may use the black hat early on in our exploration of an idea in order to find the weaknesses. We find these weaknesses in order to overcome them and put them right. When using the black hat to find weaknesses, our goal is to improve upon the idea.

We may use the black hat at the end of an exploration to make an assessment or judgment. When we want to decide on the value of an idea or when we are about to put an idea into action, then we need the black hat to be sure we are not making a mistake. In this final assessment, we can also follow the black hat with the red hat.

After our judgment, how do we now feel about the idea?

Overuse

The black hat is a valuable hat— possibly the most valuable of all— but it can be overused. There are people who only want to use the black hat. They only want to criticize ideas. They feel that this is enough. But it is not.

We need critical thinking, but we also need thinking that is creative, generative, and productive. Where are the ideas and suggestions going to come from? Criticizing ideas may improve them but does not produce new ideas. That is why the teaching of critical thinking by itself is insufficient.

Critical thinking and the black hat have a very important role to play in thinking, but by themselves they are not enough. This is not meant as a rejection of critical thinking but an observation that other kinds of thinking are also needed. One particular wheel on a car may be a very fine wheel, but one wheel alone is not enough to carry the car.

Summary of the Black Hat

The key words to describe the uses of the black hat are *checking* and *checking out.* We can check for evidence, logic, feasibility, impact, fit, and weaknesses. The two main purposes for using the black hat are finding weaknesses and making assessments. The overall question to ask is *"What is wrong with this?"*

Follow these steps to introduce the black hat: lead-in, explanation, demonstration, practice, and elaboration.

Lead-in

Begin by showing the students examples of things that have something wrong with them. Give examples with mistakes that your students will recognize. At least at first, the errors must be obvious. Following are sample errors.

Their is a place where know-one goes.

$$3 + 1 = 5 \qquad 7 + 9 = 15$$

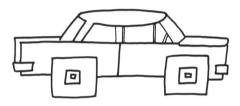

In all cases, ask repeatedly, "What is wrong with it?" After the easy examples, offer some harder ones. Lead the students to the feeling of making an effort to find out what is wrong. It is this effort that is important for black hat use. Mistakes are not always obvious.

For variety, ask students to create their own examples of things that have weaknesses or errors. Then have students trade items and examine them to discover what is wrong.

To complete the lead-in, make the reproducible **All-Weather Bike** activity on page 34 available to the students. Read the directions and the advertisement aloud, then give students time to jot down their thoughts. Invite students to share their comments with the class. Discussion notes are provided on page 35.

All-Weather Bike

Directions: Read the advertisement below. Then write what you think might be wrong with the design of the all-weather bike. Identify the weaknesses in this new kind of bicycle.

 *All-Weather Bike*

New! All-weather bike has brightly colored umbrella to protect rider from rain, sleet, snow, wind, and sun. No more wet hair or ruined clothes. Ride in comfort no matter what the forecast! Just $149.99; some assembly required.

_____

_____

_____

_____

_____

_____

_____

_____

Edward de Bono / Six Thinking Hats for Schools / 3-5 Resource Book

All-Weather Bike · Discussion Notes

Sample black hat comments:

The umbrella would stick up and could snag on things.

A gust of wind might catch the umbrella like a sail and throw the bicycle off balance.

The front of the umbrella hangs over the front wheel instead of covering the rider, so that part is wasted.

Rain, sleet, snow, and wind might blow in from the side and hit the rider.

The "assembly" of this bicycle might be more difficult than it sounds.

Accept other comments which point out weaknesses or dangers of the all-weather bike.

All-Weather Bike

Directions: Read the advertisement below. Then write what you think might be wrong with the design of the all-weather bike. Identify the weaknesses in this new kind of bicycle.

All-Weather Bike

NEW

New! All-weather bike has brightly colored umbrella to protect rider from rain, sleet, snow, wind, and sun. No more wet hair or ruined clothes. Ride in comfort no matter what the forecast! Just $149.99; some assembly required.

34

Explanation

After helping the children discover some weaknesses in the bicycle design, draw attention to the fact that they have been using the black hat.

"When we are checking to see what is wrong, we are using black hat thinking."

"If I ask you to put on a black hat, I will be asking you to see what is wrong with an idea."

It is important to keep repeating the term *black hat thinking.* This is because the formality and artificiality of the hat system is its greatest value. It is this that allows an instant switch of thinking—as deliberate as changing gears on a bicycle.

Demonstration

After introducing the black hat, make **The Open Door** reproducible on page 37 available to the students. Read the dialogue aloud or invite two students to act it out. Then give students time to identify the characters' black hat remarks and add some lines to the dialogue. Discussion notes are provided on page 38.

After discussing the dialogue, encourage volunteers to share the new lines they have written. Help the class find the black hat ideas in these lines.

For an extension to this activity, ask students to write a new scene in which characters are using black hat thinking. When students have completed their dialogues, ask volunteers to find partners and read or act out what they have written for the class.

The Open Door

Directions: Read the dialogue below. Then underline all the black hat remarks. (Remember, the black hat is for thinking about weaknesses or dangers.)

After you've underlined the black hat thinking, add one more comment that each character might make. Try to include black hat thinking in the new lines you write.

> Tony and Amy have spent a quiet night at the movies. But when they return home, they suddenly face a tough problem.

Tony: Our front door is open. There must be burglars inside. Let's call the police.

Amy: Maybe we left the door open. If people called the police every time they forgot to close their door, the police would get very annoyed.

Tony: But maybe we didn't leave the door open. If burglars are in there, we'll walk right into them!

Amy: Let's wait here and see if anyone comes out.

Tony: It's cold out here, and we might have to wait for a long time. We could make some noise to let the burglars know we're here. That would give them a chance to get away.

Amy: Then we wouldn't catch them, and they might disappear with all of our things.

Tony: Or they might be angry and try to come after us. Maybe we should go over to the neighbor's and watch our house from there to see what happens.

Amy: _____

_____

Tony: _____

_____

The Open Door · Discussion Notes

In this scene, Amy and Tony both use black hat thinking. They also use other hats, but focus students' attention on their black hat comments.

There may be some disagreement about whether a comment is black hat (weakness) or white hat (fact). Ask students to view factual comments as black hat when the facts point out a weakness in a suggestion. (See below.)

Tony: Our front door is open. *(Simple fact: white hat)* There must be burglars inside. *(Points out a danger: black hat)* Let's call the police. *(New idea: green hat)*

Amy: Maybe we left the door open. If people called the police every time they forgot to close their door, the police would get very annoyed. *(Points out weaknesses in Tony's assumption and suggestion: black hat)*

Tony: But maybe we didn't leave the door open. If burglars are in there, we'll walk right into them! *(Points out a danger: black hat)*

Amy: Let's wait here and see if anyone comes out. *(New idea: green hat)*

Tony: It's cold out here, and we might have to wait for a long time. *(Points out a weakness: black hat)* We could make some noise to let the burglars know

we're here. That would give them a chance to get away. *(New idea: green hat)*

Amy: Then we wouldn't catch them, and they might disappear with all of our things. *(Points out a danger: black hat)*

Tony: Or they might be angry and try to come after us. *(Points out a danger: black hat)* Maybe we should go over to the neighbor's and watch our house from there to see what happens. *(New idea: green hat)*

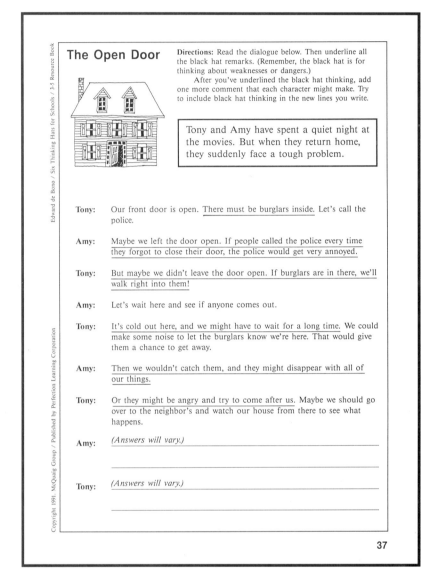

The Open Door

Directions: Read the dialogue below. Then underline all the black hat remarks. (Remember, the black hat is for thinking about weaknesses or dangers.)

After you've underlined the black hat thinking, add one more comment that each character might make. Try to include black hat thinking in the new lines you write.

Tony and Amy have spent a quiet night at the movies. But when they return home, they suddenly face a tough problem.

Tony: Our front door is open. There must be burglars inside. Let's call the police.

Amy: Maybe we left the door open. If people called the police every time they forgot to close their door, the police would get very annoyed.

Tony: But maybe we didn't leave the door open. If burglars are in there, we'll walk right into them!

Amy: Let's wait here and see if anyone comes out.

Tony: It's cold out here, and we might have to wait for a long time. We could make some noise to let the burglars know we're here. That would give them a chance to get away.

Amy: Then we wouldn't catch them, and they might disappear with all of our things.

Tony: Or they might be angry and try to come after us. Maybe we should go over to the neighbor's and watch our house from there to see what happens.

Amy: *(Answers will vary.)*

Tony: *(Answers will vary.)*

Edward de Bono / Six Thinking Hats for Schools / 3-5 Resource Book

Copyright 1991. McQuaig Group / Published by Perfection Learning Corporation

37

Black Hat Practice

In the lead-in and demonstration, you worked through some
activities with the class as illustrations of black hat thinking.
The exercises on pages 40-41, **Put On Your Black Hat,** are
for the students to tackle on their own. Students may work
as individuals or in groups (four or five students). A suggested time is given for each exercise. It is better to interrupt
students before they are finished with an item than to give
more time than needed.

Read selected tasks to the students, or reproduce the
pages so that each student has a copy. If students have their
own copies, you might invite them to select which items they
would like to try.

Help students complete the exercises by keeping time for
them. After time is up on an exercise, invite students to
share their thinking with the class.

Put On Your Black Hat

1. It is suggested that if a bike rider breaks bicycle safety rules, a big red stripe should be painted on the bike's frame. This would show that the rider is dangerous. People would not want their bikes painted, so they would ride more carefully. Do some black hat thinking on this idea.

    Suggested time: 2 minutes.

2. Do some black hat thinking to find the weaknesses in each of the following arguments.

    Choose as many topics as you wish.
    Suggested time: 1 minute per item.

    I have two tall friends, both of whom are lazy. I think all tall people are lazy.

    You should only lend money to people you don't like. Then you can be really nasty to them if they don't pay you back.

    If I can watch TV at home when I am absent from school, then it makes sense to be absent as much as possible.

Edward de Bono / Six Thinking Hats for Schools / 3-5 Resource Book

Put On Your Black Hat

3. What would happen if we made the following changes? Use black hat thinking to check out difficulties and dangers.

   Choose as many topics as you wish.
   Suggested time: 2 minutes per item.

   What if you had an extra eye in the back of your head?

   What if you could tell exactly what other people were thinking about you?

   What if only the smartest students had to go to school?

   What if the price of many kinds of foods doubled?

   What if you had to put money into your TV set to watch all programs?

4. Someone has suggested that all young people over the age of eight years must hold a paying job for five hours a week. That way they get used to the idea of working. Do some black hat thinking on this. How many black hat points can you find? What are they?

   Suggested time: 3 minutes.

5. People talk about each other a great deal. Sometimes the things they say are true, sometimes untrue, and sometimes partly true (or exaggerated). People enjoy gossiping in this way, but what are the dangers and difficulties? Do some black hat thinking on this.

   Suggested time: 3 minutes.

6. Tasha and Nikki are thinking of ways they can earn money to buy a new video game. They both make suggestions, and they both wear their black hats to think about the weaknesses of each idea. Write a dialogue between the two showing what they might say. See if you can write a scene where each character speaks at least three times.

   Suggested time: 8 minutes.

Elaboration

During the practice session, you and your students may have made additional observations on how the black hat is used. After the practice session, invite students to notice the ways they use the black hat in real life and for what purposes. These observations could be recorded in a journal and shared in subsequent class discussions. You might keep your own journal and share your uses of the black hat with the group. Journaling can help your students begin to view themselves as a community of thinkers.

For further uses of the six thinking hats in the classroom, see pages 139-160 for sample applications.

Conclusion

The black hat has many checking functions. We can check for evidence, logic, feasibility, impact, fit, and weaknesses. By using the black hat, we can find weaknesses and make assessments. In general, the black hat asks, *"What is wrong with this?"*

Yellow can mean sunshine and optimism and looking on the bright side of things. It is important, however, to make clear to students at the beginning that the yellow hat must be logical; you must give supporting reasons. If you are just expressing a general feeling of optimism or just hope that something will work, then that is not yellow hat at all but red hat thinking, which covers feelings.

If anyone suggests an idea or proposes a change, then there is usually a reason for this. It is not a random suggestion. There must be benefits for someone in the suggestion. A solution to a problem has the benefit of removing the problem. Giving food to starving people removes the hunger. Removing a pin upon which you have been sitting removes the pain.

So with the yellow hat, two questions can be asked:

What are the good points here?

What are the benefits here?

Very often the yellow hat deals with the future. A suggestion is made, a solution is offered, a plan is put forward. The benefits that are claimed for each of these are going to come about in the future. Because it is the future, we cannot be absolutely sure about anything. But we must have good reasons for claiming that these benefits will come through.

The yellow hat can also apply to the past. For instance, we might want to find the benefits of something that happened long ago or just last week.

The yellow hat is discussed in more detail on pages 44-45. Activities for teaching the yellow hat begin on page 46.

THE YELLOW HAT

What are the good points here?

What are the benefits here?

43

TEACHER NOTES · Yellow Hat

The following description is intended to serve as background for teacher reference. Consult it when needed to clarify how the yellow hat may be used and overused.

Uses of the Yellow Hat

The uses of the yellow hat can be divided into four areas, which overlap quite a bit:

1. Good points

2. Benefits

3. Reasons why an idea will work

4. Likelihood

The following sections discuss these areas in more detail.

Good Points

With the yellow hat, we think of the good points in an idea or situation. The good points of a design could be called the "strong points."

The good points may not be enough to ensure that something will work or prove to be a good choice. Suppose we see a car that is a wonderful green color—we think this color is a good point. But the inside of the car is cramped and the car uses too much fuel. Suddenly, the green color seems irrelevant.

It is important to be able to pick out the good points even when there are very few or there are many more bad or dangerous points. If the good points are of great value, we may decide that it is worth coping with the difficulties or risking the dangers in order to pursue the idea.

Benefits

Yellow hat thinking is a deliberate effort to find benefits—just as a hungry fox makes a great effort to hunt prey or a goat on a rocky mountainside spends all day looking for tufts of grass to eat. This effort is important because the benefits may not be obvious. Trying to find them may turn up benefits that no one else has noticed. That sort of thinking has been the basis for many a fortune.

There is also a need to look at how the benefits arise and at the nature of the benefits. Do the benefits arise from some special circumstances over which we have no control (for example, an anonymous benefactor donates money to buy more books for the library)? Also, are the benefits likely to be long lasting? They may depend on some circumstance which will soon change. But even if the benefits are short-lived, we may still value them.

Another essential question is, who gets the benefits from an idea? It is normal for the person who suggested the idea to benefit. A scientist may enjoy the satisfaction of having developed a new theory or may be involved in the profits of patenting an idea for a new invention.

In many cases, it is also usual for the person on the receiving end of the idea to benefit. A politician suggests a new law. This must benefit those who are going to vote for the politician. The politician in turn benefits from increased prestige and also future votes.

In addition to the benefits for the initiator and receiver of the idea, there also may be benefits to third parties. The decision to build a new school in a town will ultimately benefit the children and teachers using the school themselves. But it will also provide more jobs in the construction industry while the school is being built. In addition, having the new school may cause more families to move into the area and improve the real estate market. So it is useful to look not only at the intended benefits but also at those that develop even if unintended.

Types of Benefits

There are many types of benefits, and it is useful to go over them from time to time. In this way, you can be more sensitive to possible benefits.

Simplicity: An idea may make something simpler, such as a simpler hypothesis or a simpler way to solve a math problem. In general, if something can be made simpler, it will benefit us by requiring less effort, being more effective, and reducing errors.

Effectiveness: Some ideas have the benefit of allowing us to achieve what we set out to do in a stronger way. The effect we get is stronger.

Efficiency: An idea that improves output without increasing input or gives the same output with less input offers a benefit.

Acceptability: It is a benefit if an idea is one that people are more likely to accept than other ideas. More people will accept the idea with less persuasion.

Opportunity: If an idea will put us in a position where there are now more opportunities, then that is a benefit.

Lower cost: It is a benefit if an idea results in less cost in terms of money, time, effort, or hassle.

Lower risk: It is a benefit if a new idea reduces dangers and uncertainties.

Increased values: If an idea brings an increase in existing values (more security, peace, better health) or offers something new that we value (new friends, new interests), then this is a benefit.

So there are many types of benefits to search for with the yellow hat.

TEACHER NOTES - Yellow Hat

Why an Idea Will Work

This is the answer to the black hat criticism: Will it work? The yellow hat must always set out the full logical reasons why something is expected to work.

"This will work because . . . "

These reasons may be based on any of the following:

information ("Statistics show that the average age is . . . ")

principles of physics, chemistry, nature, etc. ("If we curve it there, it will be stronger.")

experience ("Whenever prices are about to go up, people always hurry out to buy more.")

plain logic ("If this investment is shared, each person pays less.")

The yellow hat thinker must be able to meet the objections of the black hat thinker. There may still remain a difference based on experience or different information, but there must be an answer to all objections.

As we shall see later, there is a big difference between green hat thinking and yellow hat thinking. Green hat thinking puts forward suggestions and possibilities. There is only a vague hint that they may work (and sometimes not even that). The purpose of the green hat is to come up with ideas or to get some proposals on the table. The yellow hat then takes each of these proposals and tries to show how it could be made to work. This aspect of yellow hat thinking is more constructive than judgmental.

Likelihood

It is difficult to be certain about the future. It is difficult to prove that a venture will work or that a proposed solution really will solve a problem. Nevertheless, entrepre-neurs do have to take initiative, and people do have to make decisions about problems. We cannot wait for certainty when there can be no certainty about the future.

Sometimes we can be reasonably sure about an idea, and when we are, then we can discuss our idea under the category of why an idea will work. At other times, we are not so sure. We can then think in terms of the degree of likelihood that something will work. Yellow hat thinking is only concerned with a high degree of likelihood (perhaps 70 percent or over). Lesser degrees of likelihood would come under the green hat, which deals in possibilities.

The yellow hat also seeks to establish the basis for likelihood with questions such as these: What is the evidence? What are the clues? What are the trends? What are the competing possibilities?

With likelihood, we are dealing in risks because something may not turn out as we had claimed or wished. There may even be danger, harm, loss, or damage involved. If this *harm* risk is low or absent, however, we might choose to go ahead with a project even if the *success* likelihood is lower than usual. If the *harm* risk is high, then we should want a much higher likelihood of success.

Purposes for Using the Yellow Hat

The three main purposes for using the yellow hat are

1. Assessing value

2. Extracting benefits

3. Making something work

First, we can use the yellow hat as part of an assessment and then move on to the black hat. The yellow hat part of the assessment involves listing the good points and the benefits in the proposal or idea.

The black hat then examines the weak points, difficulties, and dangers. Using the yellow hat in this way is part of making a judgment.

Second, the yellow hat can be used in a deliberate effort to extract some benefit or good points from something which has generally been thought unworkable, unattractive, or even a disaster. This yellow hat activity is not going to result in an assessment. What is extracted may, however, be of value. It is a sort of "mining" use of the yellow hat.

Third, the yellow hat can be used in an effort to make something work. This is the constructive use of the yellow hat. For example, after the green hat has put forward possibilities, the yellow hat may seek to give these a solid basis. This is an active process, not just an assessment. The constructive use of the yellow hat also seeks to establish likelihood.

Overuse

It is possible to be overly optimistic and "Pollyanna" in attitude. It is possible to believe that something will work only because you wish it to work. Or it is possible to be too optimistic as to likelihood.

Another type of overuse is to focus entirely on the yellow hat and to ignore the valuable contribution of the black hat.

Summary of the Yellow Hat

The key words to describe the uses of the yellow hat are *good points, benefits, workability,* and *likelihood.* The three main purposes for using the yellow hat are to make assessments, extract benefits, and think of ways to make something work. The overall questions to ask are *What are the good points?* or *What are the benefits?*

Follow these steps to introduce the yellow hat: lead-in, explanation, demonstration, practice, and elaboration.

Lead-in

Begin by asking students to consider the following:

What are the good points of being tall? (You can see farther; you can reach higher; you may look older.)

What are the good points of being short? (You can hide in a crowd; you can pretend to be younger; you won't bump your head in the doorway.)

If dogs could be taught to speak, what would the benefits be? (They could take and give messages; might be better company; could tell us what they see.)

What are the benefits of learning cursive handwriting? (You can write faster and with less effort; your writing looks more graceful; you can add more individual style to your writing.)

Parrots can often live to be 100 years old. What are the benefits? (A parrot can be your lifelong friend; it can be passed down to your children, like an heirloom.)

A forest is destroyed by fire. What are the benefits? (The fire provides employment for firefighters; all the old deadwood and brush is cleared away; free news coverage promotes the area.)

In all cases, ask repeatedly, ''What are the good points?'' or ''What are the benefits?''

For variety, ask students to create their own examples of things that have good points or benefits. Then have students trade items and examine them to discover the good points.

To complete the lead-in, make the reproducible **Handy Andy** activity on page 47 available to the students. Read the directions aloud, then give students time to jot down their thoughts. Invite students to share their comments with the class. Discussion notes are provided on page 48.

Handy Andy

Directions: Look at the drawing below and notice in what way Andy is different from other people. Then write what you think might be some advantages of being like Andy.

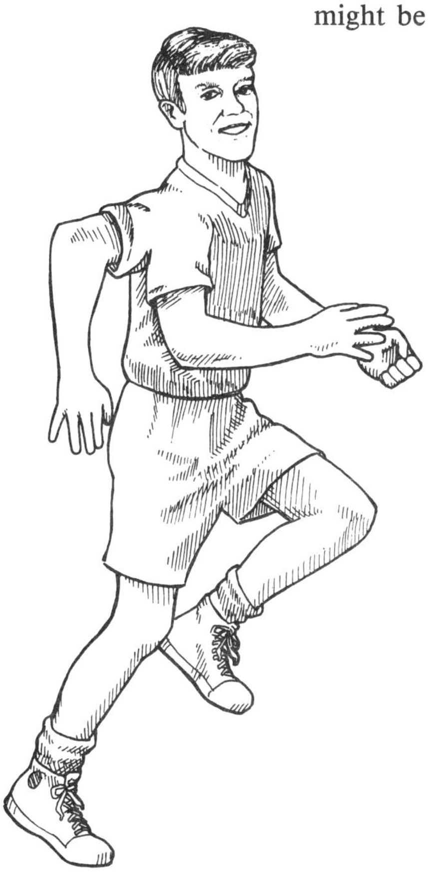

_____

_____

_____

_____

_____

_____

_____

_____

_____

_____

_____

_____

_____

_____

_____

_____

Handy Andy · Discussion Notes

Sample yellow hat comments:

The hand could be used as a spare hand in case of injury.

You could hold something while working with the other two hands.

You could hang on to scaffolding or a ladder while using the other two hands to work.

You could get a better grip on objects that you wanted to hold or lift.

You could carry more items at once.

Accept other answers that describe the benefits of having three hands.

Handy Andy

Directions: Look at the drawing below and notice in what way Andy is different from other people. Then write what you think might be some advantages of being like Andy.

47

Explanation

After helping the students discover some benefits of having three hands, the yellow hat can be introduced.

"When we are finding the benefits, we are using yellow hat thinking."

"If I ask you to put on your yellow hat, you will be looking for the good points about an idea."

As with the black hat, it is important to keep repeating and emphasizing the *yellow hat.* The more the yellow hat label is attached to the process of seeking to find benefit, the more this process can be switched on deliberately.

A comparison can be made with the black hat, but avoid a simple "good points" and "bad points" comparison. The black hat is for checking what is wrong and pointing out difficulties and dangers. The yellow hat is for good points, benefits, and why something will work out.

Demonstration

After introducing the yellow hat, make the **Two for One** reproducible on page 51 available to the students. Read the dialogue aloud or invite two students to act it out. Then give students time to identify the characters' yellow hat remarks and add some lines to the dialogue. Discussion notes are provided on page 52.

After discussing the dialogue, encourage volunteers to share the new lines they have written. Help the class find the yellow hat ideas in these lines.

Alternate Demonstration Activities

1. Ask students to write an original scene in which characters are using yellow hat thinking. When students have completed their dialogues, ask volunteers to find

partners and read or act out for the class what they have written. Help the class find the yellow hat ideas in these lines.

2. Ask students to review the **All-Weather Bike** handout which they received when learning the black hat. Invite them to wear their yellow hats and find some good points about the all-weather bike.

Edward de Bono / Six Thinking Hats for Schools / 3-5 Resource Book

Two for One

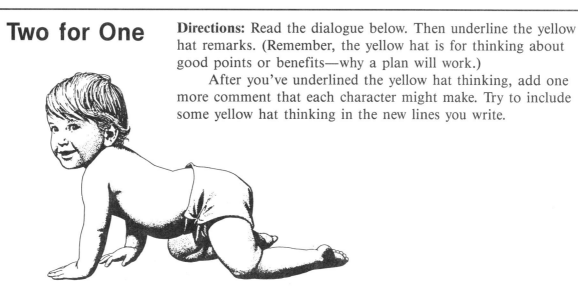

Directions: Read the dialogue below. Then underline the yellow hat remarks. (Remember, the yellow hat is for thinking about good points or benefits—why a plan will work.)

After you've underlined the yellow hat thinking, add one more comment that each character might make. Try to include some yellow hat thinking in the new lines you write.

Josh: I'm bored—I wish we had a new video game. How could we earn the money to buy a new game?

Maria: Maybe we could baby-sit. There are lots of families with little children in this neighborhood.

Josh: But we're only ten. They'll think we're too young for the job.

Maria: But the older kids are too busy to baby-sit. My older sister turns down jobs all the time. Maybe someone would give us a chance.

Josh: It might work if we said we would both sit at the same job—two sitters for the price of one. That way we'd be offering extra hands and eyes to make up for being younger.

Maria: And I could ask my sister to recommend us for jobs that she can't take. People who trust my sister would be more likely to hire us than those who don't know us.

Josh: She could tell them that I have two younger sisters that I sit for—so I'm experienced.

Maria: _____

_____

Josh: _____

_____

Two for One · Discussion Notes

In this scene, Josh and Maria both use yellow hat thinking. They also use other hats, but focus attention on finding the yellow hat comments.

There may be some disagreement about whether a comment is yellow hat (good point) or white hat (fact). Ask students to view factual comments as yellow hat when they are offered in support of a good point. (See below.)

Josh: I'm bored—I wish we had a new video game. How could we earn the money to buy a new game?

Maria: Maybe we could baby-sit. *(New idea: green hat)* There are lots of families with little children in this neighborhood. *(Fact used as good point: yellow hat)*

Josh: But we're only ten. They'll think we're too young for the job. *(Points out a weakness: black hat)*

Maria: But the older kids are too busy to baby-sit. My older sister turns down jobs all the time. *(Facts used as good points: yellow hat)* Maybe someone would give us a chance. *(Yellow hat)*

Josh: It might work if we said we would both sit at the same job—two sitters for the price of one. *(New idea: green hat)* That way we'd be offering extra hands and eyes to make up for being younger. *(Facts used as good points: yellow hat)*

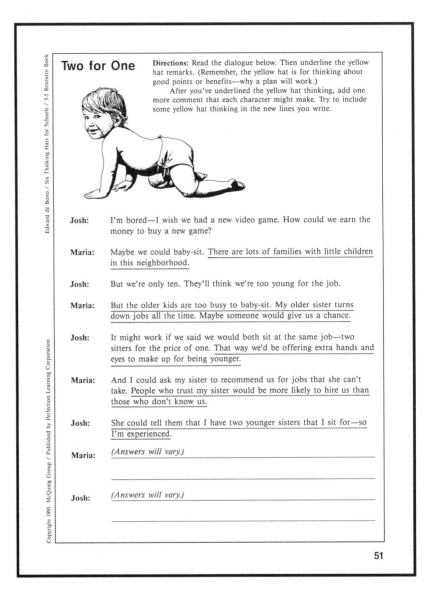

Two for One

Directions: Read the dialogue below. Then underline the yellow hat remarks. (Remember, the yellow hat is for thinking about good points or benefits—why a plan will work.)

After you've underlined the yellow hat thinking, add one more comment that each character might make. Try to include some yellow hat thinking in the new lines you write.

Josh: I'm bored—I wish we had a new video game. How could we earn the money to buy a new game?

Maria: Maybe we could baby-sit. <u>There are lots of families with little children in this neighborhood.</u>

Josh: But we're only ten. They'll think we're too young for the job.

Maria: But <u>the older kids are too busy to baby-sit. My older sister turns down jobs all the time. Maybe someone would give us a chance.</u>

Josh: <u>It might work if we said we would both sit at the same job—two sitters for the price of one. That way we'd be offering extra hands and eyes to make up for being younger.</u>

Maria: And I could ask my sister to recommend us for jobs that she can't take. <u>People who trust my sister would be more likely to hire us than those who don't know us.</u>

Josh: <u>She could tell them that I have two younger sisters that I sit for—so I'm experienced.</u>

Maria: *(Answers will vary.)*
_____

Josh: *(Answers will vary.)*
_____

Edward de Bono / Six Thinking Hats for Schools / 3-5 Resource Book

Copyright 1991. McQuaig Group / Published by Perfection Learning Corporation

51

Maria: And I could ask my sister to recommend us for jobs that she can't take. *(New idea: green hat)* People who trust my sister would be more likely to hire us than those who don't know us. *(Yellow hat)*

Josh: She could tell them that I have two younger sisters that I sit for—so I'm experienced. *(Fact used as good point: yellow hat)*

Yellow Hat Practice

As with the black hat, the exercises on the next two pages are for the students to tackle on their own. Students may work as individuals or in groups (four or five students). A suggested time is given for each exercise.

Read selected tasks to the students, or reproduce the pages so that each student has a copy. If students have their own copies of the exercises, you might invite them to suggest which items they would like to try.

Help students complete the exercises by keeping time for them. After time is up on an exercise, invite students to share their thinking with the group.

Put On Your Yellow Hat

1. The maker of a new brand of ice cream allows everyone under the age of 15 years to have all the ice cream they want for one day. Do some yellow hat thinking on this. Who will benefit? What are the benefits?

    Suggested time: 2 minutes.

2. Someone suggests putting a large hook on the roofs of cars. Why do you think that idea was suggested? Use yellow hat thinking to list some possible good points.

    Suggested time: 2 minutes.

3. What is the likelihood of each of the following ideas working out as intended? Do some yellow hat thinking on each and give the reasons why you think the plan is likely to work out. If you do not think the plan will work, just say that it won't.

    Choose as many topics as you wish.
    Suggested time: 1 minute per item.

    We should increase the number of police officers in order to reduce crime.

    Students should be paid to do schoolwork so that they will work harder.

    Shops should stay open later at night so that they could do more business.

    Restaurants should put more salt in the food so that people will get thirsty and drink more.

Edward de Bono / Six Thinking Hats for Schools / 3-5 Resource Book

Put On Your Yellow Hat

4. A restaurant decides to charge by time instead of by food. You can eat as much as you like, but you are charged a fixed fee for every fifteen minutes you are in the restaurant. Do some yellow hat thinking on this idea. List the benefits and reasons why you think the plan might work. Then do some black hat thinking to list the difficulties or problems—why it may not work. Finally, decide whether you think the restaurant has a good idea.

    Suggested time: 5 minutes.

5. List as many yellow hat points as you can think of for the following idea: Everybody must give a party once a year.

    Suggested time: 2 minutes.

6. Your cat has had four kittens. Do some yellow hat thinking on this.

    Suggested time: 2 minutes.

Elaboration

During the practice session, you and your students may have made additional observations on how the yellow hat is used. After the practice session, invite students to notice the ways they use the yellow hat in real life and for what purposes.

These observations could be recorded in a journal, as was suggested in the black hat lesson. Students might also wish to record their efforts to use the yellow hat-black hat sequence when making an assessment. Invite the class to trade journals, read, and comment on each other's entries.

For further uses of the six thinking hats in the classroom, see pages 139-160 for sample applications.

Conclusion

Yellow hat thinking finds good points, looks for benefits, tells why an idea might work or succeed, and estimates likelihood. By using the yellow hat, we can make assessments, extract benefits, and think of ways something could work. The questions to ask with the yellow hat are *What are the good points?* or *What are the benefits?*

The white hat is for finding information. Visualize the white color of a typed report, a computer printout, or a newspaper. The white hat is for neutral, objective information. There are no suggestions, ideas, or arguments. Feelings do not come into it. Just information.

Thinking is no substitute for information. If we need to know the air travel schedule between New York and Los Angeles, we look up the schedule. Thinking about it is not going to help. If we had perfect information about a matter, then thinking would be unnecessary.

The effort to find the information base (what information do we have?) and to increase the information base (what information do we need?) are key parts of thinking. They should be treated as part of thinking and not as something separate.

School is often concerned with reactive thinking. Something is put in front of the students and they are asked to react to the material. In real life, thinking is very often proactive. This means that the information is not put in front of us but we have to go out and collect it ourselves.

The white hat provides the thinker with an opportunity to focus directly and exclusively on information. The white hat also allows a thinker to ask someone else (or others in a group) to focus on information.

"Never mind the arguments. What is the information here? Let's have some white hat thinking."

However, white hat thinking is not just a matter of taking facts out of a reference book and putting them onto the table. Where does this information come from? Is it relevant? What else do we need? Thinking is involved.

In ordinary thinking, we are using information all the time and we do not need to put on a white hat to bring some piece of information into our thinking. The purpose of the white hat is to provide a means for directly focusing on information from time to time. The white hat also allows us to be clear about the information that we need but do not yet have.

The white hat is discussed in more detail on pages 58-60. Activities for teaching the white hat begin on page 61.

THE WHITE HAT

What information do we have?

What information do we need?

How do we get the information we need?

TEACHER NOTES · White Hat

The following description is intended to serve as background for teacher reference. Consult it when needed to clarify how the white hat may be used and overused.

Uses of the White Hat

The main uses of the white hat can be summarized as three questions:

1. What information do we have?

2. What information do we need?

3. How do we get the information we need?

We can visualize ourselves as explorers wearing the white hat to make a map. We fill in the areas which are known and identify the areas where more information is needed.

Information We Have

A good place to begin when using the white hat is to make note of all the information, formal and informal, that is readily available. What information do we have? The answer will give us an inventory.

Formal kinds of information can include reports, statistics, and facts. There are also "informal" kinds of information which arise from personal experience.

"Bill told me that he does not like to travel."

Describing our own feelings on a subject is red hat thinking. But reporting how others have said that they feel is white hat thinking. In such a case, we are reporting what we know—in this case, we know what Bill said—and not putting forth our own feelings.

While looking at the information that we have, we could ask other questions:

What is relevant?

What is most important?

How valid is this?

Assessing the relevance and importance of information is not easy to do at the beginning. If certain courses of action or possibilities arise, we may want to go back and look at the information again. New events and new knowledge can change the relevance and importance of information. So an early assessment of these matters is only tentative. The information must be kept available in case this assessment has to change. Otherwise, we shall simply be reinforcing the ideas with which we started out.

As we are gathering information, we may find reason to challenge its validity. If information is not true or correct, it simply should not be used. So along the way, we should be asking if our information is true or correct.

Challenging the validity of the information is important. However, a full challenge to the validity of information is a matter for black hat thinking: checking evidence, checking logic, and so forth. This black hat challenge is not carried out during the white hat thinking. Instead, there are three things that can be done:

1. Note the challenge and return to it later with specific black hat thinking.

2. Note the disagreement or doubt so that this becomes part of the information.

3. Jot down the original and the differing information so that both versions are available. If the issue becomes important later, both can be checked out.

For example, someone claims that the number of murders per year in the United States is 28,000 and someone else claims it is 15,000. We record both versions and then get on with white hat thinking.

In this way, the flow of white hat thinking continues. If there is a constant switching between white and black hats, the process becomes very messy. So proceed to make the map, but put question marks where needed.

In Japanese prints and Chinese paintings, the space is as important as the figures. In white hat thinking, we need to focus on the information that is not there. We need to be aware of and define the gaps in the information. What is missing?

Information We Need

In Japanese prints and Chinese paintings, the space is as important as the figures. In white hat thinking, we need to focus on the information that is not there. We need to be aware of and define the gaps in the information. What is missing?

A *gap* is not the same as a *need*. For instance, in a series of annual files, some years may be missing. This would be a gap in information. It may turn out that missing information is not needed. However, we should be in the habit of noting gaps in information. With *needs,* we are conscious that

TEACHER NOTES · White Hat

we do need the information and it is not there:

"We don't have enough information to make a decision. We need to know how much plan B would cost."

As with the relevance and importance of information, needs are not easy to assess at the beginning. In fact, we can probably assess them only in a general way.

"Before starting to think about this matter, we need to know the following things."

This statement is a general assessment of information needed.

In classic detective stories, white hat thinking is always featured. The great detective typically defines a crucial piece of information that will solve the case. In the same way, as our thinking about a situation unfolds, we constantly check new ideas against available information. By checking, we may find an information need that was not apparent at the beginning. It suddenly becomes vital to know something.

Needs should always be defined as specifically as possible, even if the need is general. There are two sorts of need:

1. We need more information in general about a particular area. "We need more information about dolphins."

2. We need to check something specific. "How many species of dolphins are there?" "Is it true that dolphins never sleep?" We need an answer or want to check whether something is true.

Getting the Information We Need

Having defined the information we need, we then set out to get it.

Basically, there are three ways of doing this:

1. By asking questions
2. By interpreting and making inferences
3. By consulting sources

Asking questions. Questions have a powerful way of focusing attention and getting information. Choosing and phrasing questions are key skills of any courtroom lawyer. These skills are also needed in using the white hat.

Two basic types of questions that will help us use the white hat are *fishing* questions and *shooting* questions. (See my *CoRT Thinking Program,* section V, published by SRA, for more information.)

Fishing questions are used when we need more information. We "fish" when we put down the bait but do not know what we shall catch:

"Can you describe the scene of the accident?"

"What else do you know about Ms. Hudson?"

Fishing questions are used when we need more information. We "fish" when we put down the bait but do not know what we shall catch.

Shooting questions are aimed at a specific target. After you fire, you know at once whether or not you have hit the target. So the shooting question is quite specific:

"How old are you?"

Shooting questions are aimed at a specific target. After you fire, you know at once whether or not you have hit the target.

"How much does this cost?"

Note too that shooting questions very often require a simple yes or no answer:

"Were you at home on Monday evening?"

"Did she sign the agreement?"

Interpreting and making inferences. With interpretation and inference, we try to extract something more from the information in front of us. This is similar to what detectives and scientists do through deduction: "If this is so, then this must also be so . . ." By a logical process, we move from the evidence or clues to some new information that is hidden within the available information.

Inference is meant to be based on logical deduction, but interpretation may be a matter of opinion. At some point, interpretation can move into green hat thinking in which we offer a possible hypothesis or explanation.

Interpretation also covers "reading between the lines" and noting points of significance. In the famous Sherlock Holmes case, *The Hound of the Baskervilles,* the fact that the dog did not bark was a key point. Likewise, if there are four people at a meeting and one of them says nothing, this too may be important. Or if certain uses of a new plastic are mentioned but a

TEACHER NOTES · White Hat

possible common use is not, this may be a significant omission.

By working to interpret and make inferences, we are able to get more information from what is available. There is a skill to doing this, and with practice, we can become adept at it.

Consulting sources. There was a time when an educated person could know almost all the knowledge there was to know. Today there is so much information and it is growing so rapidly that there is no way anyone can know it all. We always need to know a certain amount of background information, but beyond that, the most important thing to know is where to go to get information.

Already, many educators realize that teaching students how to get information has become a key function of education. This is happening not only at the university level but at the elementary and secondary levels as well. The framework of the white hat can be used to reinforce this point: If the information is not in front of us, and if we can't extract the information by questions, inference, and interpretation, then we have to go to some source. Here are a few basic sources.

Experts: These are people who know a lot about a subject. An expert may give the required answer or direct us to another expert or some other source.

Printed matter and audiovisual materials: There are standard references and journals in just about every field. Likewise, there are some excellent films, videos, or audiocassettes that contain a wealth of information. Many of these sources can be discovered through libraries. Knowing how to use a library, then, can open many doors.

Computer data banks: Today much information has been put on computers and can be obtained by entering the right network and asking questions. In the future, this access to information will become more valuable and convenient.

Today there is so much information and it is growing so rapidly that there is no way anyone can know it all . . . The most important thing to know is where to go to get information.

Purposes for Using the White Hat

The two main purposes for using the white hat are to

1. Stimulate thinking

2. Check thinking

At the beginning of many thinking tasks, we need information to get started. This information, in turn, will help us develop ideas (green hat thinking). At any subsequent point in our thinking, we can go back to the information to stimulate further ideas. This is like the scientist who uses the results from an experiment to form a hypothesis. We need information to start thinking. Without information, there could be no thinking.

Once we have the ideas, however, we need to see whether or not they are workable in the situation. So we go back to look at the available information. For example, a business

would do market research to see if there is a market for a new product. An archaeologist who has formed a theory about civilization X will look around to see if the available information and/or evidence supports that theory. The difference between a wild idea and a practical one is that the practical idea fits the available information; the wild one does not.

Overuse

It may seem impossible that there could be overuse of the white hat. How could we have too much information?

However, there are times when some people will refuse to do any thinking. They will just ask for more information in the hope that this information will do the thinking for them. This, of course, is not always practical. For instance, a doctor may need to act as a matter of urgency, such as in the case of suspected meningitis. It is impractical to wait for the test results because then it may be too late to save the patient. In another example, a businessperson may want to move quickly on an idea. If he or she waits until all the information is obvious, then it will also be obvious to the competitors. There are times, then, when the white hat should be put aside.

Summary of the White Hat

Some key words to keep in mind when teaching the white hat are *information, gaps, needs, questions, interpretation,* and *sources.* The two main purposes for using the white hat are to stimulate thinking and to check thinking. The basic questions to keep in mind when using the white hat are these three: *What information do we have? What information do we need? How do we get the information we need?*

Follow these steps to introduce the white hat: lead-in, explanation, demonstration, practice, and elaboration.

Lead-in

Begin by asking students to review the two hats which they have previously learned: the black hat, for checking out weaknesses and dangers, and the yellow hat, for looking at the good points and benefits.

Then invite the students to participate in some activities which will introduce another of the six thinking hats. Do not name the hat until after the lead-in is completed.

Choose from the following activities:

Tell students that you are thinking of an object, and ask them to guess what it might be. Invite them to ask any questions they like. But explain that you will only answer "yes" if the answer is yes and that you will answer "no" to all other questions.

> Example: "I am thinking of something round and flat. Ask me your questions and try to guess what the object might be." (It could be a plate, a pancake, a hamburger, a Frisbee, etc.)

Ask students to write down five points of information about their classroom—but not about the people in the room. Encourage them to look around as much as they like. Then ask volunteers to read their information aloud.

Help the students to distinguish between facts and other kinds of points like feelings, opinions, and suggestions. For instance, "I love the view from our windows," (red hat) could be reworded to make it a neutral point: "The room has windows with a view of the front lawn." "The room is terribly hot and crowded," (black hat) could be rephrased: "The desks and bookcases take up most of the floor space. The temperature in the room is 76°F."

Invite volunteers to tell all the information they know about a selected well-known person, such as a political leader or sports celebrity. Write each fact on the chalkboard or overhead as it is offered. (Do not accept opinions, suggestions, or speculation—only known facts.)

Ask students to write a topic on a sheet of paper. Then have students trade papers and list at least five facts about the topic they receive.

As the discussion for any of these activities unfolds, ask questions which repeat the words *information* and *facts*:

"What information do we have?"

"What other facts do you know?"

To complete the lead-in, give students a copy of the **New Kid on the Block** activity on page 63. Read the directions aloud, then give students time to jot down their thoughts. Invite students to share their comments with the class. Discussion notes are provided on page 64.

New Kid on the Block

Directions: Suppose that a new family has just moved into your neighborhood. You have learned that there is a child in the family. What information would you want to know about this child?

_____

_____

_____

_____

_____

_____

_____

_____

_____

_____

_____

New Kid on the Block · Discussion Notes

Sample white hat questions:

Is it a girl or a boy? How old is the child? What grade is he or she in? What school will he or she attend? Does this person have neat toys/games/play equipment? Does this person like to skateboard, swim, shop, etc.? Does this person know how to draw/build models/ride a horse/etc.? Does this person like school? How tall is this person? What color hair does this person have? Where did this person live before moving here?

Accept other questions that ask for information about the new kid. Distinguish between questions for information and questions that would elicit opinion.

New Kid on the Block

Directions: Suppose that a new family has just moved into your neighborhood. You have learned that there is a child in the family. What information would you want to know about this child?

Edward de Bono / Six Thinking Hats for Schools / 3-5 Resource Book

Copyright 1991. McQuaig Group / Published by Perfection Learning Corporation

63

Explanation

After helping the students think of questions that ask for information, the white hat can be introduced.

> "Which hat do you think we have been using today? When we are finding information, we are using white hat thinking."

> "If I ask you to put on your white hat, you will be looking for the facts about a subject."

As with the previous hats, it is important to keep repeating and emphasizing the *white hat*. Explain that the white hat is for looking at the information we have and getting more information. Contrast the black and yellow hats which are for examining ideas and suggestions.

Use this analogy: The white hat is for assembling the ingredients for cooking. The black and yellow hats are for tasting what has been cooked.

Demonstration

After introducing the white hat, make the **Skateboard Supreme** reproducible on page 67 available to the students. Read the dialogue aloud or invite two students to act it out. Then give students time to identify the characters' white hat remarks and add some lines to the dialogue. Discussion notes are provided on page 68.

After discussing the dialogue, encourage volunteers to share the new lines they have written. Help the class find the white hat ideas in these lines.

Alternate Demonstration Activities

1. Suggest that the students imagine they are planning a party for a friend. Invite them to put on their white

hats and tell what information they will need in order to plan the party.

2. Suggest that the students imagine someone is going to give them a pet for their birthday. Have students use their white hats to think of information they would want to know about the pet.

3. Ask students to review the **All-Weather Bike** handout which they received when learning the black hat. Invite them to wear their white hats and make statements that tell only the observable, neutral facts about the all-weather bike. They might also list questions that they would like answered about the bike.

Skateboard Supreme

Directions: Read the dialogue below. Then underline the white hat remarks. (Remember, the white hat is for thinking about what information you know or want to find out.) If a remark points out a fact (white hat) that could also be viewed as a good point (yellow hat), underline it. But do not underline remarks that do not contain facts.

After you've underlined the white hat thinking, add one more comment that each character might make. Try to include some white hat thinking in the new lines you write.

Brian: That's a great skateboard! It turns sharper than mine and you can jump higher on it. Where did you get it?

Aaron: I got it at Martel's. It's brand new.

Brian: I really like the design. Did they have a big selection?

Aaron: Yeah, they had some neon-colored ones and some with glow-in-the-dark grip tape. And they had some like last year's with stripes on the bottom.

Brian: How much did yours cost?

Aaron: One hundred dollars.

Brian: Is it lighter than your old one?

Aaron: Yeah, much lighter. Want to try it out?

Brian: _____

_____

Aaron: _____

_____

67

Skateboard Supreme · Discussion Notes

In this scene, Brian and Aaron both use white hat thinking. Some of their comments could be categorized as both white and yellow hat. Point out that the directions ask students to label all factual comments as white hat, even when the fact is also a good point.

Brian: That's a great skateboard! *(Emotion: red hat)* It turns sharper than mine and you can jump higher on it. *(Fact: white hat; also a good point: yellow hat)* Where did you get it? *(Request for information: white hat)*

Aaron: I got it at Martel's. It's brand new. *(Facts: white hat)*

Brian: I really like the design. *(Emotion: red hat)* Did they have a big selection? *(Request for information: white hat)*

Aaron: Yeah, they had some neon-colored ones and some with glow-in-the-dark grip tape. And they had some like last year's with stripes on the bottom. *(Facts: white hat)*

Brian: How much did yours cost? *(Request for information: white hat)*

Aaron: One hundred dollars. *(Fact: white hat)*

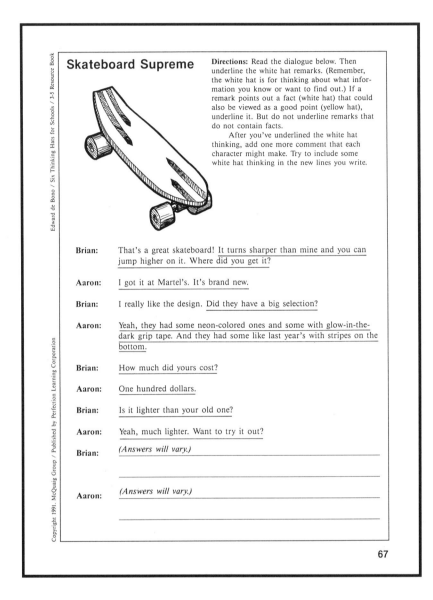

Edward de Bono / Six Thinking Hats for Schools / 3–5 Resource Book

Copyright 1991. McQuaig Group / Published by Perfection Learning Corporation

Skateboard Supreme

Directions: Read the dialogue below. Then underline the white hat remarks. (Remember, the white hat is for thinking about what information you know or want to find out.) If a remark points out a fact (white hat) that could also be viewed as a good point (yellow hat), underline it. But do not underline remarks that do not contain facts.

After you've underlined the white hat thinking, add one more comment that each character might make. Try to include some white hat thinking in the new lines you write.

Brian: That's a great skateboard! It turns sharper than mine and you can jump higher on it. Where did you get it?

Aaron: I got it at Martel's. It's brand new.

Brian: I really like the design. Did they have a big selection?

Aaron: Yeah, they had some neon-colored ones and some with glow-in-the-dark grip tape. And they had some like last year's with stripes on the bottom.

Brian: How much did yours cost?

Aaron: One hundred dollars.

Brian: Is it lighter than your old one?

Aaron: Yeah, much lighter. Want to try it out?

Brian: *(Answers will vary.)*

Aaron: *(Answers will vary.)*

67

Brian: Is it lighter than your old one? *(Request for information: white hat)*

Aaron: Yeah, much lighter. *(Facts: white hat)* Want to try it out? *(Request for information: white hat)*

White Hat Practice

Students may work as individuals or in groups (four or five students) on the following activities. A suggested time is given for each exercise.

Read selected tasks to the students, or reproduce the page so that each student has a copy. If students have their own copies of the exercises, you might invite them to suggest which items they would like to try.

Help students complete the exercises by keeping time for them. After time is up on an exercise, invite students to share their thinking with the group. Help students focus on neutral information, not on feelings, suggestions, or solutions.

Put On Your White Hat

1. Describe yourself by giving just five true statements. Each statement must cover just one fact about you.

   Suggested time: 3 minutes.

2. Describe something you own by giving five true statements.

   Suggested time: 3 minutes.

3. A friend asks you to go on vacation with his or her family. You can ask only five questions about the trip, and each question must cover only one point. What five questions would you ask?

   Suggested time: 2 minutes.

4. A friend wants you to help her sell soft drinks at baseball games. Put on your white hat to see what information you should have in order to be successful. What do the two of you need to know?

   Suggested time: 4 minutes.

5. What information would you need in order to find out more about a career or job? Put on your white hat and list the questions you might ask and who you would ask. Also write down what sources you might consult to get the answers.

   Suggested time: 4 minutes.

6. A person you do not know very well offers to sell you a camera at a low price. What white hat information do you need?

   Suggested time: 4 minutes.

Elaboration

During the practice session, you and your students may have made additional observations on how the white hat is used. After the practice session, invite students to notice the ways they use the white hat in real life and for what purposes.

Invite students to record in their journals their uses of the white hat. (See page 42.) Continue to give students time during class to trade journals, read, and comment on each other's entries.

For further uses of the six thinking hats in the classroom, see pages 139-160 for sample applications.

Conclusion

White hat thinking maps out what information is known and what information is needed. By using the white hat, we can stimulate thinking and check thinking. When wearing the white hat, we ask three questions: *What information do we have? What information do we need?* and *How do we get the information that we need?*

THE GREEN HAT

What ideas do we have?

The green hat is for creative thinking. We can look at the word *creative* in two ways. The first way means "generating, producing, creating something which was not there." The second way means "having new ideas, fresh ideas, and ideas that have not been used before." The green hat covers both aspects.

The color green brings to mind nature and vegetation. Green can symbolize productive energy or abundance. Think of shoots and branches and alternatives.

Black hat and yellow hat thinking are not enough because they are for "reactive" thinking. We use these hats to react to something that is put before us. We judge or assess it. But we need another kind of thinking to generate ideas. We can't judge or assess an idea until someone has generated it.

The green hat indicates a creative attitude. This means moving forward to possibilities and new ideas. Contrast this with description, analysis, and judgment. All of those are concerned with *what is now* rather than with *what may be next.*

The green hat deals with possibilities. At the moment we put forward an idea, it is only a possibility. Then we proceed to develop the idea and to check it out against the information and against our objectives.

We bring in the yellow hat and black hat thinking to strengthen the idea. Finally we assess the idea and compare it to alternative ideas. The generative green hat stage is the possibility stage. This is the stage of suggestions and proposals.

The green hat is discussed in more detail on pages 73-74. Activities for teaching the green hat begin on page 75.

TEACHER NOTES · Green Hat

The following description is intended to serve as background for teacher reference. Consult it when needed to clarify how the green hat may be used and overused.

Green Hat Situations

There are many types of thinking situations which call for the green hat.

Action. We are faced with a problem or we have set ourselves a task. What do we do? With green hat thinking, we can generate alternative solutions or alternative courses of action. We might do this by analyzing the problem or looking at similar problems. Or we might try using creative thinking.

Explanation. Something has happened. People have behaved in a certain way, there are scientific observations—what is the explanation? With green hat thinking, we put forward a possible explanation or hypothesis. Then we seek to check this out.

The purpose of the explanation is ultimately to allow us to move forward. We seek to explain an illness in order to see how we might treat, cure, and prevent that illness. If we can explain what motivates students to learn, then we might know how to design better strategies for teaching them.

Forecasting. It is difficult to be certain about the future. So we have to imagine possibilities. We can use green hat thinking to create alternative scenarios or future states of the world, community, family, or our own lives.

Whenever we make a decision, there are consequences. We need to be able to look at these possible consequences before we act. At this specific point, the black hat does some green hat thinking. It imagines possible future dangers and difficulties.

Design. In design and invention, we produce something new to fit a need. Using the green hat, we generate possible designs and then examine them in terms of aesthetics, cost, function, and ease of manufacture. Designers rarely come up with only one design. Many design possibilities are usually considered.

Hypothesis, Speculation, Provocation, and Lateral Thinking—Fundamentals of the Green Hat

When wearing the green hat, we use words like *suppose, maybe, perhaps, what if,* and *possibly.* All these indicate a possibility and a lack of certainty. We leap ahead of the information and lay out a possible idea. Using the new idea, the mind can view the situation in a new way.

The need to find ways to leap ahead is very important. The mind can only see what it is prepared to see. This is because of the way the mind works as a self-organizing information system. (For more detail on this point, see my book *I Am Right—You Are Wrong.*) Three ways to move ahead of the existing information are by forming hypotheses, speculating, and making provocative statements.

A hypothesis is supposed to be the most reasonable explanation. A scientist uses green hat thinking to generate a hypothesis. This hypothesis is then checked out by designing experiments to show that the hypothesis is wrong. The more a scientist and colleagues fail to disprove a hypothesis, the stronger it becomes.

A speculation is less reasonable than a hypothesis. It involves more guesswork.

"What if we look at it this way . . . "

"What if this was not caused by heat but by the increased noise . . . "

"Suppose the murderer did not flee as everyone believes. Suppose he or she is still around?"

A provocation goes even beyond speculation. Provocations help us dislodge our minds from their usual patterns. (See my book *Lateral Thinking* published by Harper & Row.) We use the special word *PO* (provocative operation) to signal a provocation.

"PO: Cars should have square wheels."

With provocation there is no pretense at reasonableness. A PO statement may appear to be complete nonsense.

Lateral thinking is a term I invented in 1967 to describe the thinking that is used to cut across the patterns of perception formed by the self-organizing behavior of the brain. The technical background for this is described in *I Am Right—You Are Wrong.* There are a number of specific lateral thinking techniques which can be used deliberately in order to generate new ideas.

One very simple technique is the use of a random word. We simply take any word (preferably a noun) and put it alongside the subject for which a new idea is needed. For example we might say "study PO frog" to get some new ideas about how to teach students better study habits. From this juxtaposition, we get the idea of having students use headings in a chapter to hop through the text, previewing the material they are going to read.

Random words are extremely easy to use. The process works because a random word allows us to enter our patterns of thinking at

TEACHER NOTES · Green Hat

a new point and so increases the chances of opening up new patterns. (For more information about the educational uses of lateral thinking, see part IV of my *CoRT Thinking Program* published by SRA.)

If the techniques of lateral thinking are known or available, they can be used as part of green hat thinking. However, the techniques are not essential since green hat thinking covers all attempts to be creative.

Purpose for Using the Green Hat

Green hat thinking is not only concerned with *new* ideas. Green hat thinking is concerned with the generation of *any* ideas. If someone comes up with a very old idea to solve a problem, this can still be green hat thinking. The main purpose of green hat thinking is to be generative, productive, and to move thinking forward. Finding completely new ideas is only one means of making progress.

Uses of the Green Hat

We can look at four main activities of green hat thinking:

1. Generating reactive ideas
2. Generating starting ideas
3. Generating further and better ideas
4. Generating new ideas

Generating Reactive Ideas

When an idea is presented, we can use the green hat in a reactive way. We can ask, "What is interesting about this idea?" The word *interesting* indicates a creative exploration to see what the idea suggests or what the idea leads to. We use the given idea as a starting point in order to explore creatively.

We can use the green hat reactively to modify or improve an idea that has been presented. We can do this even before the black hat has pointed out weaknesses in the idea.

> "That is a good idea, but it would be even better if we let people choose their own reward."

Generating Starting Ideas

On our own or as part of a group, we set out to think about something. We use the white hat first to collect the information. Then what? We need some starting ideas. The green hat is used to lay out some starting ideas. Sometimes the starting ideas are easy, obvious, and conventional. Sometimes it is difficult to get any ideas at all.

These starting ideas do not have to be proven or sure things before they can be put forward. They are only possibilities. Such ideas are then checked against the information and developed with yellow hat and black hat thinking.

Generating Further or Better Ideas

There are times when we do have some ideas, but they do not seem very satisfactory. We may not be able to choose between the obvious alternatives because none of them seems of great value. So instead of pushing ahead with the existing ideas, we make an effort to see if there are further ideas and further alternatives. We may never find them, but we make the effort.

> "We seem to be bogged down here. Let's put on our green hats and try to find some new approaches."

Even when there is no obvious need to look for further alternatives, it is a good thinking habit to make some effort to see if there might be other ideas. Quite often an idea seems satisfactory but with a little effort a much better idea can be found. There is no reason at all to suppose that the first satisfactory idea you find is the best solution to the problem.

Generating New Ideas

There are times when we really do want new ideas. This may be for reasons of competitive advantage: we need new products; we want to set up a new business. It may be because the old ways simply do not work any longer. In either case, we specifically set ourselves the task of generating *new* ideas. This is where the deliberate techniques of lateral thinking could be used (such as the random word *technique*).

Overuse

Creativity and the green hat can be overused. To ignore sound conventional ideas and to search only for new and exotic ideas may be an overuse of the green hat. To want to work only in the area of possibilities and to refuse to come down to practical realities is also overuse. To continue to look for further ideas when immediate action needs to be taken is overuse. To wait for a magic new idea to solve all problems is also overuse.

The green hat, like all the other hats, has its role, its place and its use. In general we do not use the green hat nearly enough, whereas we tend to overuse the black hat.

Summary of the Green Hat

Some key words related to the green hat are *creative, generative, possibilities,* and *alternatives.* Green hat thinking can help when we need to take an action, provide an explanation, forecast an outcome, or design something new to fit a need. Forming hypotheses, speculating, and thinking laterally are three green hat thinking tools. We use the green hat to generate reactive ideas, starting ideas, further ideas, and new ideas. The overall question for green hat thinking is *What ideas do we have?*

Follow these steps to introduce the green hat: lead-in, explanation, demonstration, practice, and elaboration.

Lead-in

Begin by making a simple outline drawing on the chalkboard or overhead projector. This might be a square with a wiggly line trailing from one of the bottom corners. Then ask the class for suggestions as to what the drawing might represent. (It might be a kite, a mouse trapped under a box, overhead view of a leaking tank, etc.)

Then make another simple drawing and ask what this could be. As students make suggestions, point out that their suggestions are *possibilities, creative ideas,* or *alternatives.* These are the sort of words you want to use to lead in to the green hat concept.

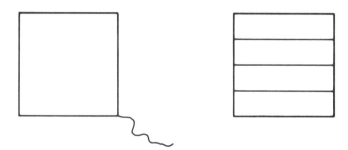

After discussing the drawings, ask students to make a diagram showing how the human head could be improved.

> "How would you improve the human head? What ideas do you have?"

Usually this produces eyes on the back of the head, octopus-like tentacles, rearrangement of the hair, bigger ears, etc. Accept all ideas without comment, since the green hat does not evaluate. Invite students to trade diagrams or display their ideas so that all can see the variety of possibilities that the class has proposed.

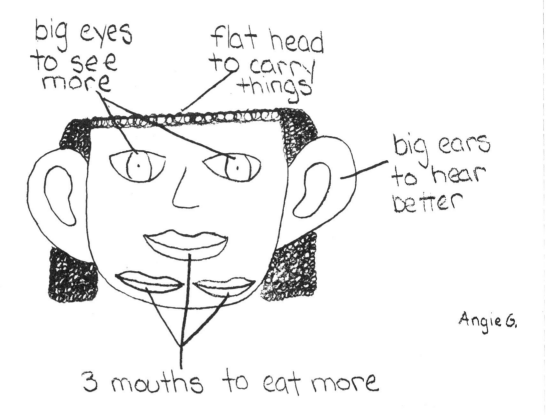

big eyes to see more

flat head to carry things

big ears to hear better

Angie G.

3 mouths to eat more

In discussing the diagrams, make comments which reinforce the features of green hat thinking and distinguish it from the black, yellow, and white hats. Do not name the green hat, however, until after the lead-in is completed.

"These are creative designs. These are suggestions. You were free to think of any possibilities. If we wanted to assess those possibilities, we would use the yellow hat and the black hat. If we wanted more facts, we would use the white hat."

To complete the lead-in, make the reproducible **Mystery Man** activity on page 77 available to the students. Read the directions aloud, then give students time to jot down their thoughts. Invite students to share their comments with the class. Discussion notes are provided on page 78.

Mystery Man

Directions: A man is walking down a busy street with a brown paper bag pulled over his head. Why is he doing this? What is going on? Write your ideas on the lines below. Try to give at least two possible explanations.

_____

_____

_____

_____

_____

_____

_____

_____

_____

_____

_____

_____

_____

_____

_____

_____

_____

Mystery Man · Discussion Notes

Sample green hat comments:

The man might be wearing the sack to win a bet.

He might be trying to see what a blind person feels like.

Maybe he doesn't like his new haircut.

It might be a publicity stunt.

He might be a walking advertisement for brown paper bags.

He might be promoting the use of recyclable packaging.

Maybe he is wearing the bag so that he won't be recognized. He might be famous, or an escaped convict. Perhaps he owes someone some money.

Accept other comments which explain why the man might be wearing the sack.

Mystery Man

Directions: A man is walking down a busy street with a brown paper bag pulled over his head. Why is he doing this? What is going on? Write your ideas on the lines below. Try to give at least two possible explanations.

Edward de Bono / Six Thinking Hats for Schools / 3-5 Resource Book

Copyright 1991 McQuaig Group / Published by Perfection Learning Corporation

77

Explanation

After discussing the possible explanations for the mystery man's behavior, explain that the students have been wearing the green hat to generate these ideas. This is the hat of *creativity, ideas,* and *possibilities*. The relationship with the green color of vegetation can be emphasized. The green hat also can be associated with new growth and energy. Encourage a free flow of ideas—we do not have to be sure that an idea is a good one before putting it forward.

The next activity introduces the random word approach (see teacher notes, page 73) as a green hat thinking tool. First, discuss the following situation with the students.

"You need to carry some water in a bucket from the kitchen into the bedroom. But you find the bucket has a hole in the bottom, so you will drip water all over the house if you use it. How can you get the water to the bedroom without making a mess? Put on your green hats and give me some solutions to this problem."

Record students' suggestions on the chalkboard or overhead. (Examples: Block up the hole with chewing gum or some other substance; lay papers on the carpet to catch the drips.) After students have offered all their suggestions, invite them to try the random word technique to generate further green hat ideas.

"There is a way of getting new ideas by using a random word. We just find any noun and use it to stimulate ideas. I'm opening the dictionary to any page and counting down to the sixth word on that page. That word is not a noun, so I'm going down the page from there—we'll use the first noun I can find—*meatball.*

"Now think of *bucket leak* and *meatball* together. Or we can say *bucket leak* PO *meatball.* PO means that *bucket leak* and *meatball* do not really fit together but we are putting them together to help us think of some new ideas. What ideas can you think of by connecting *bucket leak* and *meatball*?"

Give students a few minutes to answer; don't be too quick to prompt them. However, if this juxtaposition stumps them, you might offer one of the following. ''We cook meatballs in a skillet—perhaps a skillet could transport the water. A meatball is circular in shape—perhaps there is a helmet in the house or a fishbowl (or other semicircular object that is not ordinarily used for carrying liquids) that could be used.''

If necessary, the technique can be tried again with another problem: bicycle PO banana. (This suggests a long banana-shaped saddle so you could sit anywhere along it; new colors you could apply to a bike but peel off when you want to change them; banana-shaped handlebars that you could grip comfortably at any point, etc.)

Demonstration

After introducing the green hat, make the **Shoes with a View** reproducible on page 81 available to the students. Read the dialogue aloud or invite three students to act it out. Then give students time to identify the characters' green, yellow, and black hat remarks. Discussion notes are provided on page 82.

Alternate Demonstration Activities

1. Ask students to write an original scene in which characters are using green hat thinking. When students have completed their dialogues, ask volunteers to find partners and read or act out what they have written for the class. Help the class find the green hat ideas in these lines.

2. Ask students to review the **All-Weather Bike** handout which they received when learning the black hat. Invite them to wear their green hats and find some ways to improve the all-weather bike.

Shoes with a View

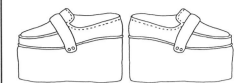

Directions: Read the dialogue below. Underline the green hat remarks. (Remember, the green hat is for thinking of possibilities—creative ideas that could be tried.) Then tell what kind of thinking each character is doing by writing the name of the character in the correct blank at the bottom of the page.

Alice: I think someone should invent a pair of shoes which are raised about four inches above the ground.

Alberto: Yes, short people could wear them and catch up a bit with taller people.

Kate: But shoes like that would be heavy and tiring to wear.

Alice: The platforms could be made out of very lightweight plastic.

Kate: It still would be difficult to walk, and running would be almost impossible.

Alberto: One good thing is that the tops of the shoes wouldn't get so dirty from puddles or mud. And you might be able to get used to running in this kind of shoe if you practiced.

Alice: Perhaps the platforms could be detachable so that you just slip the bottoms off when you want to run.

Alberto: They could be fun shoes. It would be fun to be instantly taller.

Kate: You might start knocking your head on the top of doorways.

_____ is wearing the **green hat.**

_____ is wearing the **black hat.**

_____ is wearing the **yellow hat.**

Shoes with a View · Discussion Notes

In this scene, Alice comes up with the ideas (green hat). Kate points out the problems (black hat). Alice finds a way of overcoming the problems which Kate brings up (more green hat). Alberto looks at the good points but does not actually suggest any creative ideas (yellow hat).

Emphasize that the thinking hats are to be put on and taken off. Alice, Alberto, and Kate could agree to trade hats. Thinkers should strive to be equally as good at wearing each of the six hats and not an expert at only one kind of thinking.

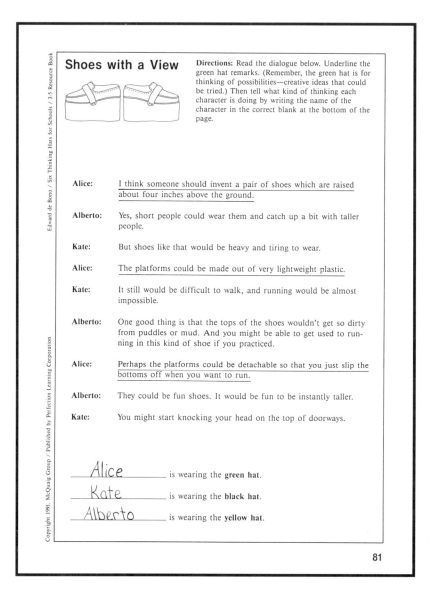

Shoes with a View

Edward de Bono / Six Thinking Hats for Schools / 3-5 Resource Book

Directions: Read the dialogue below. Underline the green hat remarks. (Remember, the green hat is for thinking of possibilities—creative ideas that could be tried.) Then tell what kind of thinking each character is doing by writing the name of the character in the correct blank at the bottom of the page.

Alice: I think someone should invent a pair of shoes which are raised about four inches above the ground.

Alberto: Yes, short people could wear them and catch up a bit with taller people.

Kate: But shoes like that would be heavy and tiring to wear.

Alice: The platforms could be made out of very lightweight plastic.

Kate: It still would be difficult to walk, and running would be almost impossible.

Alberto: One good thing is that the tops of the shoes wouldn't get so dirty from puddles or mud. And you might be able to get used to running in this kind of shoe if you practiced.

Alice: Perhaps the platforms could be detachable so that you just slip the bottoms off when you want to run.

Alberto: They could be fun shoes. It would be fun to be instantly taller.

Kate: You might start knocking your head on the top of doorways.

Alice is wearing the **green hat**.

Kate is wearing the **black hat**.

Alberto is wearing the **yellow hat**.

81

Green Hat Practice

The exercises on the next two pages are for the students to tackle on their own. Students may work as individuals or in groups (four or five students). A suggested time is given for each exercise.

Read selected tasks to the students, or reproduce the pages so that each student has a copy. If students have their own copies of the exercises, you might invite them to suggest which items they would like to try.

Help students complete the exercises by keeping time for them. After time is up on an exercise, invite students to share their thinking with the group.

Note: Four hats are now available. At this point, physical hats or other color indications can be freely used. Display the hat of appropriate color to indicate the type of thinking required.

Such concrete signals are fun, but they also serve to reinforce the concept of role-playing and role switching, which is very important. Each hat symbolizes a request for a deliberate and specific thinking effort. Providing tangible symbols helps students distinguish between the various strategies they are learning. "When I put on *this* color of hat (pick up this flag, hold this colored square, step in this colored circle, sit on this colored bean bag, etc.), I do *this* kind of thinking. And when I change colors, I change to a new kind of thinking."

Put On Your Green Hat

Edward de Bono / Six Thinking Hats for Schools / 3-5 Resource Book

1. What is *interesting* about the following things? What creative uses might you suggest for each?

    Choose as many topics as you wish.
    Suggested time: 1 minute per item.

    an airplane that can fly very slowly

    a cup with a handle on both sides

    a book which is numbered backward so that it begins with the highest number and ends with page one

    a cat with no fur or hair

2. Use the word *cornflakes* to generate some new ideas for a TV game show.

    Suggested time: 3 minutes.

3. A starting idea is any suggestion given to get thinking started. Starting ideas do not have to be logical or practical, but may lead to other ideas which are more usable. Give some starting ideas to help change each of the following situations.

    Your parents have the volume on the TV set turned up very high, and you can't do your homework.

    There are too many stray cats in the neighborhood.

    Someone is making fun of you.

    Suggested time: 2 minutes per item.

Put On Your Green Hat

4. In what way could you improve an ordinary pencil? Use your green hat and the word *mouse* to help you get ideas (pencil PO mouse). When you have an idea, use yellow hat thinking to make that idea as strong and as practical as possible.

   Suggested time: 2 minutes green hat,
   2 minutes yellow hat.

5. Two inventors, Mike and Diana, have invented a talking yo-yo. They are trying to persuade a manufacturer (Sam) to produce the yo-yo. At the meeting, Mike is wearing a green hat, Diana is wearing a yellow hat, and Sam is wearing a black hat. Write what they say at the meeting. Each person should talk three times, and there should be a conclusion.

   Suggested time: 15 minutes.

6. Give some possible explanations for each of the following situations. Use your green hat thinking to put forward possibilities.

   Why do people spray-paint graffiti on public property?

   Why is there no school on Saturdays in the United States?

   Why do some students work harder than others?

   Suggested time: 2 minutes per item.

Elaboration

During the practice session, you and your students may have made additional observations on how the green hat is used. After the practice session, invite students to notice the ways they use the green hat in real life and for what purposes.

These observations could be recorded in the students' journals. Invite the class to trade journals, read, and comment on each other's entries.

For further uses of the six thinking hats in the classroom, see pages 139-160 for sample applications.

Conclusion

Green hat thinking generates ideas for action, provides explanations, forecasts outcomes, and offers new designs. By using the green hat, we can generate reactive ideas, starting ideas, further ideas, and new ideas. The green hat asks *What ideas do we have?*

The red hat is worn to express the thinker's feelings, emotions, hunches, and intuitions. Think of the redness of fire. Think of anger and joy but also of warmth and contentment. The red hat includes both intense and more gentle feelings.

When reporting feelings, the thinker may say, "This is what I feel." No justification or explanation or logical support is required.

The red hat covers the feelings at this moment in time: "This is what I feel right now." It may be that in a few minutes the feelings will be different as a result of further information or a perception change.

Feelings, emotions, hunches, and intuitions are all very real, but they are not based on visible logical deduction. They are often based on experience and familiarity with a subject, just as we recognize a friend's face from the total picture. At times it is not even possible to explain the feeling: "I have a strong feeling about this project—but I cannot tell you why."

If we are not permitted to put forward our feelings, we simply disguise them as logic and create a rationalization for them. We are then committed to supporting that rationalization. The red hat helps prevent this kind of deception.

Feelings are an important part of thinking. Outside of mathematics and similar "game systems," most thinking involves feelings. Even an objective scientist will have a feeling about the elegance of a theory or a hunch about the inadequacy of evidence (in addition to the fiercer emotions directed towards a rival's work).

We cannot put feelings to one side and pretend that thinking should always be objective and free of feeling. Without feelings, values would have little power, and without values, thinking would be inhuman. It also would be almost impossible to make choices.

Used at the right place, feelings are what decides the value of the thinking for ourselves as individuals or for society as a whole. Used at the wrong point, though, feelings can wreck thinking. Strong feelings at the beginning of the thinking (jealousy, fear, anger) so limit perception that thinking can only be used to support these feelings.

The value of the red hat is that it recognizes feelings, emotions, hunches, and intuitions as a valid part of thinking and at the same time labels them for what they are.

The red hat is discussed in more detail on pages 89-90. Activities for teaching the red hat begin on page 91.

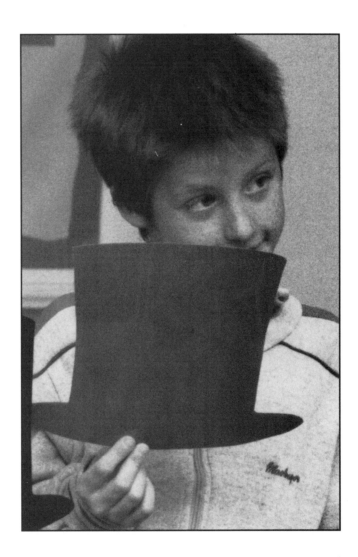

TEACHER NOTES · Red Hat

The following description is intended to serve as background for teacher reference. Consult it when needed to clarify how the red hat may be used and overused.

Shades of Red Hat Thinking

The spectrum of feelings included under the red hat ranges from emotions to intuitions.

Emotions. Here we have normal emotions such as joy, anger, fear, jealousy, and sorrow. Under the influence of these powerful emotions, our perception selects only what supports the emotion. A jealous person will see reasons for jealousy. An angry person will see reasons for anger.

Feelings. This is a general term and covers a much wider range than emotions. There may be feelings of unease or uncertainty. There may be feelings of anxiety. There may be a feeling of potential or of interest. Aesthetics is a feeling. So is the camaraderie that develops when a group works together. The term *feeling* is so broad that it even covers matters like admiration and respect.

Hunches. A hunch lies somewhere between a feeling and an intuition. It takes the form of a strong feeling or decision in favor of or against something. No valid explanation of this decision is available to the person with the hunch. A hunch is something like the vision of a prophet. The hunch seems very real to the person with the hunch, and he or she feels the need to tell others.

Intuitions. There is a claim that intuition is indeed a logical process but that we are not consciously aware of this process. There may be merit to this claim. Intuition may also be the result of complex experiences in the field. It may not be possible to make conscious all the aspects of this experience.

Intuition is often right, but it can also be disastrously wrong. For example, intuitions about probability are notoriously wrong. How many people have lost money gambling when their intuition tells them they are bound to win on the next throw?

Validation of Feelings

The value of the red hat is that it recognizes emotions, feelings, hunches, and intuitions as a valid part of thinking, provided they are signaled as what they are. We can accept an intuition if it is offered as an intuition and not as a logical deduction. We can accept a feeling if it is put forward as such.

The value of the red hat is that it recognizes emotions, feelings, hunches, and intuitions as a valid part of thinking.

Because the device of the red hat makes feelings legitimate, there is no need to apologize for the fact that it is *only* a feeling. Nor—and this is important—is there ever any need to explain or rationalize the feeling. The feeling or intuition now has a validity in its own right: "In spite of all that argument and black hat thinking, I still like the idea."

Focus

Feelings can be focused. A thinker can express a feeling about the total situation or only one part of it: "I like your agenda for the planning session, but I am not happy about having it on May 5."

A thinker may have positive feelings about one aspect of the situa-tion and negative feelings about another. Both these can be put forward provided the focus is given.

Range

It is possible to express a wide range of feelings that vary from the crude to the very subtle. We can like or dislike an idea. We might find an idea attractive or appealing or we might find an idea unattrac-tive or unappealing. We can be happy with an idea or unhappy.

There is also a range of feelings which express unease, uncertainty, and disquiet. These are not as strong as disliking an idea, but we are moving in that direction. We need to be reassured.

We may find an idea boring. This is not to say that it is a bad idea or that it will not work—but just that we do find it boring. It is important with the red hat to realize that feelings must always be subjective. The idea itself is not boring, but *we* find it boring.

The opposite of boring is ex-citing, interesting, or stimulating. These feelings imply that the idea has potential. It is not just the pre-sent form of the idea that is being considered, but all the possibilities opened up by the idea. The idea may not be workable in its present form, but it can still be interesting.

In the end we can probably nar-row all these different feelings down to four:

"I like the idea."

"I don't like the idea."

"I am uncertain about the idea."

"I find the idea interesting."

Mixed Feelings

It is legitimate for us to say that we have mixed feelings if this is the case. However, to say that we have mixed feelings as a way of avoiding making our feelings public is not

TEACHER NOTES · Red Hat

legitimate. Most listeners will recognize the escape. In some circles the term *mixed feelings* very clearly indicates that the speaker does not like the idea at all and is politely expressing disapproval.

At times we simply may have no feelings about a matter. If so, we can just report that we do not have any red hat thinking to offer.

Uses of the Red Hat

There are two main uses of the red hat:

1. Making feelings known

2. Making assessments and choices

Making Feelings Known

At any moment we may signal that we are putting on the red hat: ''Putting on my red hat, I am unhappy about the demands the community is placing on our schools.''

We could have put forward the same feelings without the red hat. It is precisely the formality of labeling the feelings with the red hat, however, that makes the feelings more acceptable.

If there are likely to be strong existing feelings about a matter, then it is helpful to begin discussion of the matter with the red hat. Someone may ask for three minutes of red hat thinking all around. This way background feelings are brought quickly out into the open.

What happens if someone is dishonest about his or her feelings? There is no objective way of checking on feelings. The listener or listeners may, however, express doubt: ''I doubt whether those are your true feelings.''

Very occasionally we may be permitted to wear the red hat on behalf of someone else. This means that we spell out what we believe the other person's feelings to be: ''I am going to put on the red hat for you and to stand in your shoes. I don't think I would like this proposal at all.''

On the other hand, if we are just reporting feelings previously expressed by others, that is not red hat but white hat thinking: ''Travis told me he is worried about his test scores.''

The red hat label can be useful in helping people become aware of what they are doing and insisting that they change their behavior: ''That is your red hat thinking—now can you switch to some other hat?'' Keep in mind, however, that the red hat is not intended to be just accusatory, but also exploratory: ''What are our red hat feelings about this suggestion?''

In general the red hat must be seen as an *opportunity* to make feelings and intuitions known and not a *demand* that these be shared.

Making Assessments and Choices

Before we put any idea into action, we have to use the black hat to be sure we are not making a mistake. The black hat checks out the idea. After this black hat thinking, we then use the red hat: ''What do I now feel about the idea?'' If the black hat shows that the idea is dangerous or unworkable, we would normally begin to dislike the idea.

There are times, however, when the black hat shows that an idea is dangerous or unworkable, but we like it anyway. In such cases, instead of dismissing the idea completely, we may set out to make the idea more workable. Or we may decide to accept the risks.

In choices or decisions, there is an assessment of each alternative with both yellow and black hats. When this has been done and when the full picture is available, then it is up to the red hat to make the final choice. Which alternative do we *like* best?

In practice we may want to recheck with the black hat: ''This is the alternative I like—let me check to see whether anything terrible would happen if I went ahead.''

Overuse

There is overuse of the red hat when we use only red hat thinking on all occasions and never do any other sort of thinking.

There is overuse of the red hat when we take up a red hat position and then refuse to look at the information or listen to arguments.

The most common overuse is when we use the red hat too frequently in the course of a discussion. The main value of the red hat is at the beginning (to make feelings known) and at the end (assessment and choice). Frequent red hat interruptions can interfere with the thinking process. Any feelings which have not changed during the course of a discussion can be put forward at the end. There is no point at all in reacting to every comment and suggestion with immediate red hat response.

Summary of the Red Hat

Some key words to describe red hat thinking are *emotions, feelings, hunches,* and *intuition*. The two main uses of the red hat are to disclose feelings and to make assessments and choices. The overall question to ask is *What do I feel about this?*

Follow these steps to introduce the red hat: lead-in, explanation, demonstration, practice, and elaboration.

Lead-in

Begin by helping students review the nature of feelings and emotions:

> "What could I say that might make each of you feel happy?" (Here is some money, you can all go home, tomorrow you're going to Disneyland, etc.)

> "What could I say that might make each of you feel unhappy?" (You must stay after school today, you have a test tomorrow, it will be your job to clean the school from now on, etc.)

> "What we are talking about is feelings and emotions. Give me some other examples of feelings that people can have." (They might feel happy, sad, jealous, frightened, angry, hungry, curious, etc. Accept all suggestions that could be considered a feeling in the broad sense. See teacher notes, page 89, for more examples.)

> "Sometimes we have a feeling that something is true, even though we can't prove that it is. We might have a *hunch* that a friend will call us. Or our *intuition* might tell us that someone is not telling the truth. Hunches and intuitions can also be considered feelings.
> "What are some hunches or intuitions that you have had?" (That it would rain today, that I would get a certain grade on a test, that something good or bad would happen, that an accused person was not really guilty, etc.)

To complete the lead-in, make the reproducible **What Are Your Feelings?** activity on page 92 available to the students. Read the directions aloud, then give students time to jot down their thoughts. Invite students to share their comments with the class. Discussion notes are provided on page 93.

What Are Your Feelings?

Edward de Bono / Six Thinking Hats for Schools / 3-5 Resource Book

Directions: For each of the following items, place a check in one column to show whether you like it, don't like it, find it interesting, or have no feeling about it.

Item	Like	Don't like	Interesting	No feeling
1. books				
2. movies				
3. dogs				
4. cats				
5. dancing				
6. sleeping				
7. swimming				
8. bowling				
9. loud music				
10. home				

What Are Your Feelings? · Discussion Notes

Invite students to compare the feelings that they indicated on their handouts. Explain that feelings can vary widely and that all feelings are acceptable. Also establish that feelings do not have to be explained or justified.

Reassure students, too, that feelings can change from moment to moment. Encourage students to feel free to report any changes in their feelings as discussions unfold.

What Are Your Feelings?

Directions: For each of the following items, place a check in one column to show whether you like it, don't like it, find it interesting, or have no feeling about it.

Item	Like	Don't like	Interesting	No feeling
1. books				
2. movies				
3. dogs				
4. cats				
5. dancing				
6. sleeping				
7. swimming				
8. bowling				
9. loud music				
10. home				

(Answers will vary.)

92

Explanation

After helping the students complete the **What Are Your Feelings?** activity, introduce the red hat. The red hat is for expressing feelings, emotions, hunches, and intuitions.

"What do I feel about this?"

"What is my hunch about this?"

Feeling is an important part of thinking, and the red hat gives us a chance to make our feelings known. The association of red with fire, anger, and warmth might help students remember the color. Point out that the red hat does not give people permission to be offensive or insulting. We just say what *we* feel. We do not accuse others of anything. ("I feel angry," *not* "I feel that you are stupid," etc.)

Demonstration

Make the **New Friends or Strangers?** reproducible on page 96 available to the students. Read the dialogue aloud or ask two students to act it out. Then give students time to identify the characters' red hat remarks. Discussion notes are provided on page 97.

Alternate Demonstration Activities

1. Explain that in many fairy stories someone finds a very old bottle on a beach. When the bottle is opened, a genie or spirit comes out of the bottle. This genie is so pleased to be released after hundreds of years inside the

bottle that the genie offers the finder a choice of three wishes. The finder can choose only one.

a. to be rich

b. to be happy

c. to be beautiful/handsome

Invite students to put on their red hats and discuss the wishes with a neighbor. Ask them to tell the neighbor their red hat feelings about each wish, then make a final choice according to their feelings.

2. Ask students to review the **All-Weather Bike** handout from the black hat lesson or the **Shoes with a View** handout from the green hat lesson. Invite them to wear their red hats and tell how they feel about the bike or the new kind of shoes. Remind them not to justify or explain their feelings.

New Friends or Strangers?

Directions: Read the dialogue below. Then underline the red hat remarks. (The red hat is for feelings and hunches.)

Kevin: Marty's birthday party is next week. I don't feel like going.

Mei Hua: Why? He's going to take everyone to the skating rink!

Kevin: I have a hunch there'll be lots of kids from his old school. I feel uneasy about that.

Mei Hua: I love to make new friends.

Kevin: Well, I hate strangers.

Mei Hua: I'd feel lost without you.

Kevin: I'm sorry. I'll let you know if my feelings change.

New Friends or Strangers? · Discussion Notes

In this scene, Kevin and Mei Hua both use the red hat. They also use other hats, but focus attention on finding the red hat comments.

After discussing the dialogue, invite students to give their own feelings about meeting new people.

Kevin: Marty's birthday party is next week. *(Fact: white hat)* I don't feel like going. *(Feeling: red hat)*

Mei Hua: Why? *(Request for information: white hat)* He's going to take everyone to the skating rink! *(Fact: white hat* or *Good point: yellow hat)*

Kevin: I have a hunch there'll be lots of kids from his old school. *(Hunch: red hat)* I feel uneasy about that. *(Feeling: red hat)*

Mei Hua: I love to make new friends. *(Feeling: red hat)*

Kevin: Well, I hate strangers. *(Feeling: red hat)*

Mei Hua: I'd feel lost without you. *(Feeling: red hat)*

Kevin: I'm sorry. *(Feeling: red hat)* I'll let you know if my feelings change. *(Fact: white hat)*

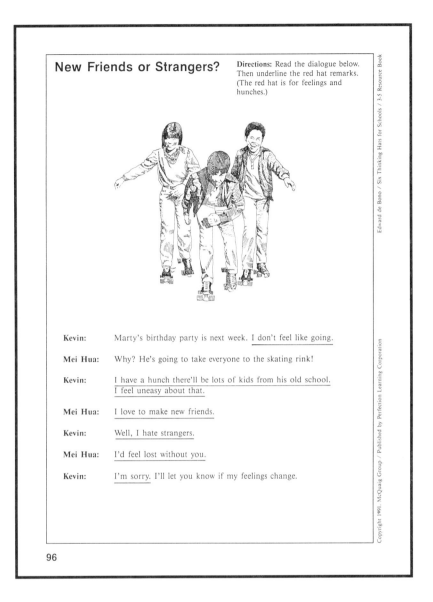

New Friends or Strangers?

Directions: Read the dialogue below. Then underline the red hat remarks. (The red hat is for feelings and hunches.)

Kevin:	Marty's birthday party is next week. I don't feel like going.
Mei Hua:	Why? He's going to take everyone to the skating rink!
Kevin:	I have a hunch there'll be lots of kids from his old school. I feel uneasy about that.
Mei Hua:	I love to make new friends.
Kevin:	Well, I hate strangers.
Mei Hua:	I'd feel lost without you.
Kevin:	I'm sorry. I'll let you know if my feelings change.

96

Red Hat Practice

The exercises on the next two pages are for the students to tackle on their own. Students may work as individuals or in groups (four or five students). A suggested time is given for each exercise.

Read selected tasks to the students, or reproduce the pages so that each student has a copy. If students have their own copies of the exercises, you might invite them to suggest which items they would like to try.

Help students complete the exercises by keeping time for them. After time is up on an exercise, invite students to share their thinking with the group.

Put On Your Red Hat

1. Put on your red hat and think about what your feelings would be if any of the following happened to you:

   You are hit by a car and break your leg.

   Someone gives you a large sum of money.

   You find that someone you thought was a friend has been saying bad things about you.

   You suddenly become very good at your favorite sport.

   You get to meet a movie star.

   Suggested time: 2 minutes total.

2. For each pair, say which you like best:

   Coca-Cola or Pepsi?

   Chocolate chip ice cream or vanilla ice cream?

   Video games or game shows?

   Loud music or not-so-loud music?

   Geography or mathematics?

   Baseball or hiking?

   Suggested time: 2 minutes total.

3. If you look into the future, what is your intuition about the following? Put on your red hat and tell what you think will happen. Remember, with the red hat you do not have to explain your feelings.

   Will there be more or fewer children?

   Will there be more or less crime?

   Will people be more or less interested in sports?

   Will the school year be shorter, longer, or about the same?

   Suggested time: 3 minutes total.

Put On Your Red Hat

Edward de Bono / Six Thinking Hats for Schools / 3-5 Resource Book

4. What if red paint were sprayed on you in these different situations? Describe what your feelings would be in each case:

   as part of a TV show

   as a practical joke played on you by your friends

   as an accident when you walked under a ladder

   as a stunt to raise funds for charity

   Suggested time: 3 minutes total.

5. There is a suggestion that all people (adults as well as young people) should wear very brightly colored clothing. Use the following sequence of hats to help you decide what you think of the idea:

   What is your final view?

   Suggested time: 3 minutes.

6. Write a scene in which three friends find a briefcase stuffed with money. They suspect the money is stolen but disagree on what to do with it. Have each character give his or her red hat thinking on the subject. Each person should speak at least three times.

   Suggested time: 15 minutes.

Copyright 1991. McQuaig Group / Published by Perfection Learning Corporation

Elaboration

During the practice session, you and your students may have made additional observations on how the red hat is used. After the practice session, invite students to notice the ways they use the red hat in real life and for what purposes.

These observations could be recorded in the students' journals. Invite the class to trade journals, read, and comment on each other's entries.

For further uses of the six thinking hats in the classroom, see pages 139-160 for sample applications.

Conclusion

Red hat thinking expresses emotions, feelings, hunches, and intuitions. We can use the red hat to disclose feelings and to make assessments and choices. The red hat asks *What do I feel about this?*

THE BLUE HAT

What thinking is needed?

What is the next step?

What thinking has been done?

The blue hat is different from all the other hats. The other hats are concerned with thinking about a particular problem, subject, or difficulty. The blue hat is for thinking about the thinking that is being used.

We can associate the blue hat with the blue sky which is above everything. If we were up in the sky, we could look down and see what was happening on the ground below. With the blue hat, we try to rise above the thinking that is taking place and to get an overview of this thinking.

With the blue hat we try to take charge of our thinking in order to organize what is going on. The blue hat is like the conductor of the orchestra who organizes what instruments are playing at any moment. There is a technical term for this kind of thinking about thinking: *metacognition.*

Using the blue hat at the beginning, in the middle, and at the end of thinking can help us make sure that the process is comprehensive and complete. In the beginning, the blue hat is used to define the focus and purpose of the task. The blue hat may also be used to put forward an agenda of thinking steps. In the middle, the blue hat restates objectives, redefines the problem, provides a summary, or decides the next step. Then at the end, the blue hat gives a final summary and then insists on a conclusion or outcome. If, for example, a summary lists five alternatives that were proposed, the conclusion will note the one that has been selected.

Note: The blue hat is discussed in more detail on pages 103-104. Activities for teaching the blue hat begin on page 105.

TEACHER NOTES · Blue Hat

Intelligent people can sometimes be poor thinkers. This is not because they cannot think but because the order in which they carry out their thinking steps is inefficient. It is like having a powerful car but driving it badly. There is nothing wrong with the car but the driver is not making the most of the car's potential.

Consider two thinkers faced with a similar situation. Here is the process each uses to manage the thinking:

Thinker A:

1. This is what I think about this matter.

2. Now I am going to prove to you that I am right.

Thinker B:

1. I want to explore the matter.

2. Here are some alternative views that are possible.

3. This is the view I prefer.

4. Now let me explain how I reached that conclusion.

With Thinker A, the conclusion comes first, and the thinking is just a defense of that conclusion. With Thinker B, there is an exploration of the subject leading to a conclusion which is then explained.

With the blue hat, we can learn to think about our thinking and to plan for better results.

Uses of the Blue Hat

The blue hat is most often used at the beginning, in the middle, and at the end of a thinking session. The five main uses include

1. Defining focus and purpose

2. Setting out a thinking plan or agenda

3. Making observations and comments

4. Deciding the next step

5. Defining outcomes and summarizing

Defining Focus and Purpose

"What are we thinking about?"

"What are we trying to do?"

"What is the desired outcome?"

If we are going somewhere, it is useful to know where we are trying to go. So the blue hat has a very important role to play at the beginning of the thinking.

The blue hat defines the problem or task and the purpose of the thinking. The blue hat lays out the situation.

If we are going somewhere, it is useful to know where we are trying to go. The blue hat defines the problem or task and the purpose of the thinking. The blue hat lays out the situation.

This initial definition of the thinking task need not be done by a single person. The group can discuss the definition with all members of the group wearing blue hats. It is usually helpful to try out several alternative definitions of the task or problem.

The thinking of a group may stray from the purpose of the thinking, or the purpose may change as the thinking unfolds. At such times, someone can put on the blue hat to restate or to redefine what the group is trying to do.

Restating means simply repeating the original thinking task to keep the thinkers on track: "May I put on my blue hat to remind you that we are trying to think of all the creatures that might live in or near a pond."

Redefining indicates a change in the task: "Putting on my blue hat, I would like to note that we have decided to stop thinking about where to have the class picnic until Julie checks on our transportation. Right now we are going to think instead about what food we would like to serve."

Setting Out a Thinking Plan or Agenda

Another blue hat function is to set out an agenda of thinking steps which are to be followed one after the other. An agenda of *subjects* is common enough at meetings. So the idea of an agenda of thinking steps is not a difficult transition.

A simple agenda might be a plan for using the thinking hats in a particular sequence. (See Sequences, page 117 ff.) But a thinking agenda is by no means confined to the use of the six thinking hats. It may cover any thinking process whatsoever.

Making Observations and Comments

Once thinking has begun, we may put on the blue hat to stand back from the thinking in order to comment upon it. The comment may be upon the thinking of another person, the group, or the thinker's own thinking.

"Putting on my blue hat, I feel that we have just been telling what is wrong with this idea, and we should now think about how to improve it."

"My blue hat thinking is that we are trying to think about two

TEACHER NOTES · Blue Hat

different things at once. Let's take one at a time.''

''I'm putting on my blue hat to say that we have just had a great deal of red hat thinking.''

The purpose of a blue hat comment is to be constructive. If we know what we are doing wrong, then we can try to put it right. It may be that the thinking has just concentrated on one part of a problem. It may be that the class has gotten bogged down in an argument between two people. The blue hat provides a mirror in which the thinkers can see their own thinking.

Deciding the Next Step

''What shall we do next?''

''What is the next step?''

It is surprising how much thinking just drifts on from one point to another. What someone says triggers an idea in someone else's mind and that in turn leads to another comment. So it continues. As long as there is no silence or gap, then everyone believes that useful thinking is being done.

The blue hat can stop this drift by making the ''next step'' a conscious decision. The blue hat can be used to propose a next thinking step that can be taken because it is useful—not just because it follows from random conversation.

''Putting on my blue hat, I feel we must have some white hat thinking here.''

''My blue hat thinking is that we list our alternatives first, and then examine each one of them.''

The next step may involve the use of one of the hats, but it can involve any other thinking step at all. It could even include making a decision to *stop* thinking for a while and take a break.

Defining Outcomes and Summarizing

''What conclusion have we reached?''

''What is the outcome?''

At the end of the thinking, we can use the blue hat to insist on an outcome. This outcome can take the form of a solution, conclusion, choice or decision, design, plan, or something else definite—like a promise or a contract.

Where the outcome is not so definite, then the blue hat tries to assess what has been achieved. Perhaps the thinkers have defined a new problem or discovered an obstacle that needs to be confronted. Or the need for some vital information has been identified. Perhaps what has been achieved is a better understanding of the matter. Or possible alternatives have been generated—even if no choice was made.

There is always an outcome of some sort, even if it is not the exact one we sought. In the end, the blue hat seeks to define this outcome, whatever it may be.

The blue hat can also be used to ask for a summary at any stage in the thinking.

''I would like to put on my blue hat and to see what we have done so far. It seems to me that we have made three decisions.''

The thinker can offer his or her own summary or can ask someone else for a summary:

''What have we got so far?''

''Where are we now?''

This request for a summary may also serve to show that very little has been achieved. The summary can then identify problems, obstacles, and information gaps.

Purposes for Using the Blue Hat

The blue hat is usually put on by the person who is suggesting its use. Unlike the other hats, we rarely ask someone else to put on a blue hat. It is possible, however, to suggest that the whole group pause and put on a blue hat to examine the thinking that is taking place or that needs to take place.

The blue hat tends to be announced and used less frequently than the other hats. People often carry out blue hat functions without feeling a need to say so. But it is worthwhile to get into the habit of using the blue hat deliberately and explicitly in order to make easier the shift to the metacognitive level (thinking about thinking).

Overuse

It is possible to belabor thinking by requiring a detailed agenda for every minor task. It is possible to make so many blue hat interruptions during a thinking task that the main purpose of the thinking is forgotten. It is possible to wear the blue hat to ''correct'' people and to tell them that they are doing something wrong. All of these are overuses of the blue hat.

Summary of the Blue Hat

The blue hat is most often used at the beginning, in the middle, and at the end of a thinking session. Some key words to describe the uses of the blue hat are *focus, purpose, agenda, observations, next step, outcome,* and *summary.* Three questions to ask with the blue hat are *What thinking is needed?, What is the next step?,* and *What thinking has been done?*

ollow these steps to introduce the blue hat: lead-in, explanation, demonstration, practice, and elaboration.

Lead-in

Ask a student to come forward and to be blindfolded. Change the nature of the room slightly (move some furniture or set up some obstacles) and then invite another student to *direct* the movements of the blindfolded person. The director must provide instructions which will enable the sightless person to walk to the back of the room without bumping into things.

As an additional activity, ask students to write instructions for making a paper hat (perhaps one of the colored hats). Invite a few students to read their instructions aloud, while someone else tries to follow them. Ask the class to decide whether the instructions are complete or if anything has been left out. The same exercise may be conducted using some other task—for example, making a hamburger or a peanut butter sandwich.

The Blue Hat

As these activities are being completed, make comments which reinforce the features of blue hat thinking and distinguish it from the other hats. Do not name the blue hat, however, until after the lead-in is completed.

> "We are thinking of instructions to help us complete the job we are trying to do. We are thinking about what we are doing, instead of just jumping in and doing it. We are making a plan."

To complete the lead-in, make the reproducible **Fox in a Fix** activity on pages 106-107 available to the students. Read the directions aloud, then give students time to complete the thinking map. Invite students to share their results with the class. Discussion notes are provided on page 108.

Fox in a Fix

Directions: Two girls are walking beside a river. One girl spots a fox caught in a trap on the opposite bank. The girls must decide what they will do, if anything, about the fox.

Below are four steps which the girls might use to think about the fox. Cut out the steps and place them on the Thinking Map to show which thinking step should come first, second, and so on.

Edward de Bono / Six Thinking Hats for Schools / 3-5 Resource Book

**Think about
what we have done.**
Did our plan work?
Why or why not?

Choose one plan.
Which plan do we want
to try? Which is safest?
Most likely to work?
Quickest? Easiest?
Best for us?
Best for the fox?

**Think of the possible
plans.** What are all the
things we could do
about the fox? (Ignore
it. Free it. Play with it.
Treat its wounds. Kill it.
Or what else?)

**Think about
getting ready to
try out the plan.**
What equipment will
we need? Whose help?
What should we do
first? Next? Last?

FOX IN A FIX - Thinking Map

This map already shows several action steps for two girls who find a fox in a trap. Place the thinking steps on the map to show which thinking step should come first, second, and so on.

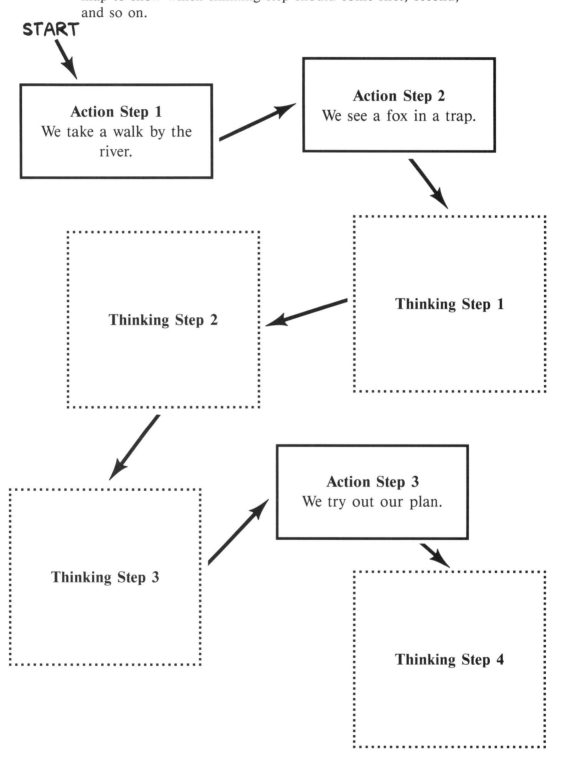

START

Action Step 1
We take a walk by the river.

Action Step 2
We see a fox in a trap.

Thinking Step 2

Thinking Step 1

Thinking Step 3

Action Step 3
We try out our plan.

Thinking Step 4

Fox in a Fix · Discussion Notes

Ask students to compare their maps and find out whether everyone placed the steps in the same order. Invite some students to explain how they designed their maps. The map at right shows a likely response. However, someone may be able to justify an alternative.

During the discussion, focus students' comments on the order of the thinking steps, rather than on the answers to the sample questions each step asks. For example, guide students away from lengthy debate about how the girls might get across the river or what should become of the fox.

Step 1
Think of the possible plans.
What are all the things we could do about the fox? (Ignore it. Free it. Play with it. Treat its wounds. Kill it. Or what else?)

Step 2
Choose one plan. Which plan do we want to try? Which is safest? Most likely to work? Quickest? Easiest? Best for us? Best for the fox?

Step 3
Think about getting ready to try out the plan. What equipment will we need? Whose help? What should we do first? Next? Last?

Step 4
Think about what we have done. Did our plan work? Why or why not?

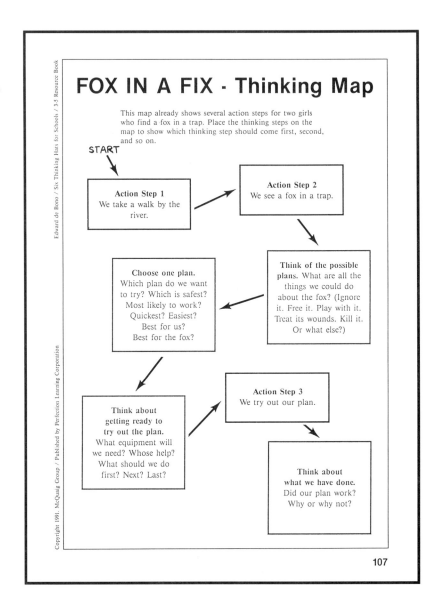

Explanation

After the **Fox in a Fix** activity has been completed, explain to students that they have been wearing the blue hat to think about thinking.

"Wearing the blue hat is like being in the sky above, looking down at a situation and planning for the best way to think about it."

"When we directed the blindfolded student, we were planning the steps to help the person reach a goal. When we built the thinking map about the fox, we were planning the steps to help the girls reach a goal too."

"The blue hat directs the thinking that is being done. The blue hat is for thinking about thinking. What kind of thinking should I do next?"

"When the six thinking hats are used, we can put on the blue hat to decide what other color hats are needed."

The other hats (black, yellow, white, green, red) can now be reviewed. The point is made that the blue hat is different from the other hats because it is not thinking about the *subject* but about the *thinking* that is needed. At the simplest level the blue hat has two functions: to look at the thinking that we are doing and to tell us what thinking to do next.

Demonstration

After introducing the blue hat, make the **Tight Squeeze** reproducible on page 111 available to the students. Read the dialogue aloud or invite two students to act it out. Then give students time to identify the characters' blue hat comments. Discussion notes are provided on page 112.

Alternate Demonstration Activities

1. Ask students to write an original scene in which characters are using blue hat thinking. When students have completed their dialogues, ask volunteers to find partners and read or act out what they have written for the class. Help the class find the blue hat ideas in these lines.

2. Suggest the following situation to students: There seems to be a thief in the classroom. Several things have been stolen. You are going to think about this situation. Put on your blue hat to decide the thinking steps. What are you going to try to do?

   Possible steps: a) think about ways to catch the thief (green hat); b) assess each alternative (yellow/black hat); c) choose the plan you like (red hat); and d) try it out (action).

   Another sequence: a) get more information about the situation (white hat); b) think of a plan to discourage or scare the thief (green hat); c) identify weaknesses in the plan (black hat); d) improve the plan (yellow/green hat); and e) try it out (action).

   Accept a variety of answers, but help students focus on planning how to think about the problem rather than just tackling the problem itself.

Edward de Bono / Six Thinking Hats for Schools / 3-5 Resource Book

Tight Squeeze

Directions: Read the dialogue below. Then underline the blue hat remarks. (Remember, the blue hat tells what thinking we are doing or what thinking should come next.)

Roy: We'll never get this piano through that door.

Jim: That's good black hat thinking, Roy. But let's put on our blue hats for a minute. How can we think about this? Let's use the green hat to think of some ways to solve the problem. Even crazy ideas—any ideas at all.

Roy: Okay. We could make the door bigger; we could tear the piano apart; we could try getting the piano through the window. We could try to find a smaller piano. We could blow a big hole in the wall with dynamite. We could forget the piano and make the chorus sing without it.

Jim: Good. Now back to the blue hat. Let's think about our goals. Our first goal is to get the piano through the door. But there's another goal—not to hurt the piano or the door or any other property. Now let's put on the black hat and see which of our ideas won't work because of our goals.

Roy: Well, we can't take the piano apart or make the door bigger or blow up the wall because all these would do damage.

Jim: Right. What thinking could we do about the idea of moving the piano through the window?

Roy: We need the yellow hat to find the good points. My uncle has a hoist we could use to lift the piano if it would fit through the window. And it would be easy to test—just measure the piano and the window.

(A few minutes later)

Jim: The piano is two inches larger than the window! Now what?

Tight Squeeze · Discussion Notes

Roy: We'll never get this piano through that door. *(What's wrong: black hat)*

Jim: That's good black hat thinking, Roy. But let's put on our blue hats for a minute. How can we think about this? Let's use the green hat to think of some ways to solve the problem. Even crazy ideas—any ideas at all. *(What thinking we are doing/what thinking should come next: blue hat)*

Roy: Okay. We could make the door bigger; we could tear the piano apart; we could try getting the piano through the window. We could try to find a smaller piano. We could blow a big hole in the wall with dynamite. We could forget the piano and make the chorus sing without it. *(New ideas: green hat)*

Jim: Good. Now back to the blue hat. Let's think about our goals. *(What thinking should come next: blue hat)* Our first goal is to get the piano through the door. But there's another goal—not to hurt the piano or the door or any other property. *(Information: white hat)* Now let's put on the black hat and see which of our ideas won't work because of our goals. *(What thinking should come next: blue hat)*

Roy: Well, we can't take the piano apart or make the door bigger or blow up the wall because all these would do damage. *(Weaknesses: black hat)*

Tight Squeeze Directions: Read the dialogue below. Then underline the blue hat remarks. (Remember, the blue hat tells what thinking we are doing or what thinking should come next.)

Roy: We'll never get this piano through that door.

Jim: That's good black hat thinking, Roy. But let's put on our blue hats for a minute. How can we think about this? Let's use the green hat to think of some ways to solve the problem. Even crazy ideas—any ideas at all.

Roy: Okay. We could make the door bigger; we could tear the piano apart; we could try getting the piano through the window. We could try to find a smaller piano. We could blow a big hole in the wall with dynamite. We could forget the piano and make the chorus sing without it.

Jim: Good. Now back to the blue hat. Let's think about our goals. Our first goal is to get the piano through the door. But there's another goal—not to hurt the piano or the door or any other property. Now let's put on the black hat and see which of our ideas won't work because of our goals.

Roy: Well, we can't take the piano apart or make the door bigger or blow up the wall because all these would do damage.

Jim: Right. What thinking could we do about the idea of moving the piano through the window?

Roy: We need the yellow hat to find the good points. My uncle has a hoist we could use to lift the piano if it would fit through the window. And it would be easy to test—just measure the piano and the window.

(A few minutes later)

Jim: The piano is two inches larger than the window! Now what?

111

Jim: Right. What thinking could we do about the idea of moving the piano through the window? *(What thinking should come next: blue hat)*

Roy: We need the yellow hat to find the good points. *(What thinking should come next: blue hat)* My uncle has a hoist we could use to lift the piano if it would fit through the window. And it would be easy to test—just measure the piano and the window. *(Good points: yellow hat)*

(A few minutes later)

Jim: The piano is two inches larger than the window! *(Information: white hat)* Now what? *(What thinking should come next: blue hat)*

Blue Hat Practice

The exercises on the next two pages are for the students to tackle on their own. Students may work as individuals or in groups (four or five students). A suggested time is given for each exercise.

Read selected tasks to the students, or reproduce the pages so that each student has a copy. If students have their own copies of the exercises, you might invite them to suggest which items they would like to try.

Help students complete the exercises by keeping time for them. After time is up on an exercise, invite students to share their thinking with the group.

Put On Your Blue Hat

1. Put on your blue hat and choose which of the other hats you would want to use first in each of the following situations:

   Choose as many topics as you wish.
   Suggested time: 1 minute per item.

   A man collapses in the street in front of you.

   Your friend is accused of cheating on a test, but you know that he or she didn't.

   You have been having a long argument with your mother, who wants you to clean up your room.

   You are at a party and your father, who was going to give you a ride home, becomes ill and cannot pick you up.

   There is a bad smell in the room.

2. Put on your blue hat and make up a plan for thinking about this problem:

   The vacant lot next door to the school is very dirty—even unhealthy. There are papers, cans, and broken bottles all over the place.

   Suggested time: 4 minutes.

3. Write a scene based on the following situation. A girl named Molly gets a box of candy as a gift from Jessica. The next day, Molly tells Jessica that when she opened the box, half the candy was gone. What do the two girls say to each other? Each character should speak three times. The blue hat must be mentioned twice.

   Suggested time: 6 minutes.

4. A neighbor has a fierce guard dog that gets out through a hole in the fence. This dog has not yet bitten anyone, but it terrifies people. Use your blue hat to tell what hats you would use to think about this situation. Then go ahead and do the thinking. Finally, summarize your thinking and tell what you would do about the dog.

   Suggested time: 10 minutes.

Edward de Bono / Six Thinking Hats for Schools / 3-5 Resource Book

Copyright 1991. McQuaig Group / Published by Perfection Learning Corporation

Put On Your Blue Hat

5.   Put on your blue hat and tell what thinking might be used to solve the following problems.

> *Choose as many topics as you wish.*
> *Suggested time: 2 minutes each.*

> You are trying to decide what to wear to a costume party.

> You have to spend an evening at home, but there are no good books to read and you have seen all the videos.

> All of your friends are going to a party, but you haven't been invited.

> You want to buy something but don't have enough money with you.

> Someone you don't like insults you.

6.   Your parents tell you that you must spend Saturday mornings working around the house. You really don't like the idea, but you want to think about it. Use your blue hat to explain what hats you will use to think about it.

> *Suggested time: 4 minutes.*

7.   The circus was planning to give three performances in the town. But a sudden storm has wrecked the circus tent. Imagine that you are the owner of the circus. Put on your blue hat and describe the thinking that should now take place.

> *Suggested time: 3 minutes.*

Elaboration

During the practice session, you and your students may have made additional observations on how the blue hat is used. After the practice session, invite students to notice the ways they use the blue hat in real life and for what purposes.

These observations could be recorded in the students' journals. Invite the class to trade journals, read, and comment on each other's entries.

For further uses of the six thinking hats in the classroom, see pages 139-160 for sample applications.

Conclusion

We most often use the blue hat at the beginning of a thinking session, in the middle, and at the end. We can use the blue hat to define our focus and purpose, to set out a thinking plan, to make observations and comments, to decide the next step, or to summarize. With the blue hat, we ask, *What thinking is needed?*, *What is the next step?*, or *What thinking has been done?*

By now we are familiar with the six hats. We've looked in detail at each hat and its uses. We know how to put on a hat and how to take it off. The hats provide an opportunity to use a certain type of thinking or to stop using it.

"Putting on my red hat, I will tell you my feelings."

"Now I think we should switch from black hat thinking to green hat thinking."

In the normal course of thinking, someone may request the use of one hat or another from time to time, but most of the thinking does not take place under any particular hat. It is important to know this, because if we try at every moment to specify a hat, the six hat method can become quite cumbersome.

In addition to putting on single hats, we can use sequences of more than one hat. Sequences provide tools for carrying through more complex thinking operations. Learning and discussing sample sequences also is an excellent way to reinforce the use of the single hats. This is because the function of a hat in a sequence illustrates the way that hat is supposed to work.

Note: Some suggested sequences are described on pages 118-122. Activities for teaching the sequences begin on page 123. The sample applications at the back of this book show the sequences in classroom applications.

SEQUENCES

Sequences provide tools for carrying through more complex thinking operations

TEACHER NOTES · Sequences

First Ideas

First Ideas is really the beginning stage of all thinking. First the blue hat defines the thinking task very clearly. Then the white hat collects the available information. The green hat seeks to put forward some possible ideas or suggestions. These do not need to be new ideas. Conventional and obvious ideas are also put forward at this stage.

First Ideas involves generative thinking while most of the other sequences are reactive. So this sequence deserves to be given some priority. It is simple but makes a big difference in thinking.

The generative stage is usually followed by an assessment.

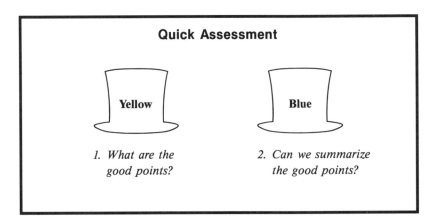

First Ideas

Blue | White | Green

1. What is the thinking task?

2. What do we know about the situation?

3. What ideas can we think of?

Quick Assessment

If there are no benefits at all in an idea or a suggestion, then there is no point in pursuing it further. The matter can be ignored or dismissed (if there is that choice). There is no point in testing feasibility because if an idea has no benefits, it does not matter whether the idea would work or not. So the yellow hat makes an effort to find benefits. The blue hat summarizes the benefits—if there are any.

Quick Assessment

Yellow | Blue

1. What are the good points?

2. Can we summarize the good points?

Evaluation

This sequence can be used when something is put before us and we judge its value.

When evaluating, it is always best to use the yellow hat before the black hat because it is difficult to be positive after we have seen all the difficulties. Using the yellow hat first may result in a positive bias, but that is not a bad thing. Because the black hat is so powerful, a positive bias can help prevent us from overlooking worthwhile ideas.

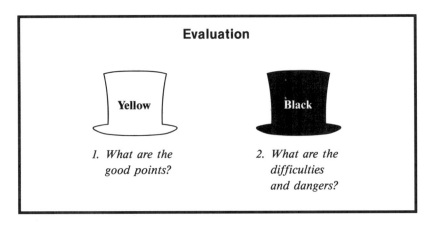

Evaluation

Yellow | Black

1. What are the good points?

2. What are the difficulties and dangers?

TEACHER NOTES · Sequences

Improvement

This sequence puts the black hat to constructive use. The black hat points out the weaknesses in a design or idea so that the idea can be improved. The green hat suggests how the improvements might be made. This particular use of the black hat does require a constructive attitude.

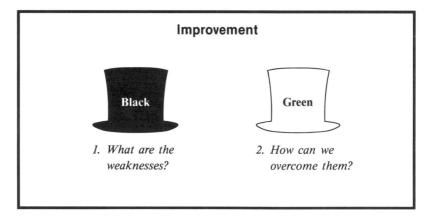

Explanation

Something has happened and an explanation is needed. The white hat spells out exactly what has happened. The green hat comes up with possible explanations for why it has happened. One of these possibilities may fit so well that it becomes the likely explanation.

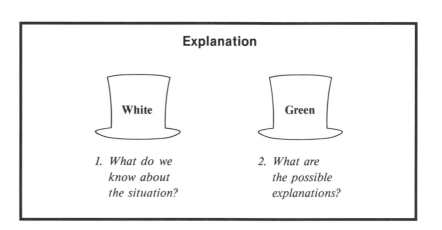

Direct Action

This sequence helps when an emotional response produces an impulsive desire to take immediate action. Before taking the action (punching a person back, for example), the black hat is brought in for a quick assessment. This helps us make sure that the action won't lead to disaster.

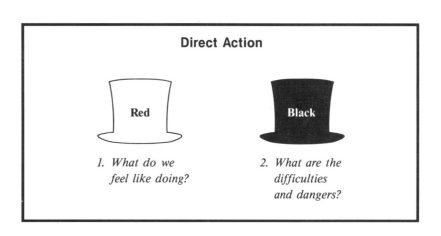

TEACHER NOTES · Sequences

Emotions

We can use this sequence when a situation arouses a strong emotional response. First we identify our feelings. Then we look at the facts about the situation. The green hat generates possible courses of action. Then the blue hat draws a conclusion.

The conclusion may be that no action is required. But if a course of action is decided upon, then that course of action needs to be assessed. This can be done with just the black hat or with the yellow/black combination.

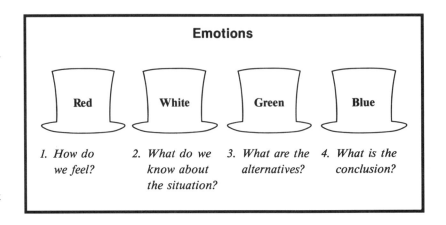

Caution

When caution is needed, we look at a situation specifically for potential dangers. This is not a full assessment of the situation but a danger-avoiding assessment.

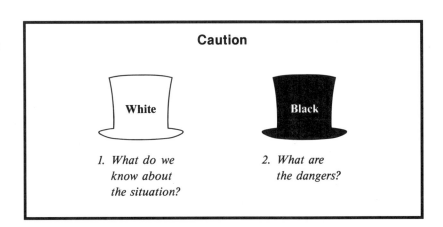

Opportunity

This hat is used to develop a habit of checking to see whether or not there is any value in a suggestion, idea, or situation. First we lay out the facts. Then we use the yellow hat to pick out points of potential benefit. This is the opposite of caution.

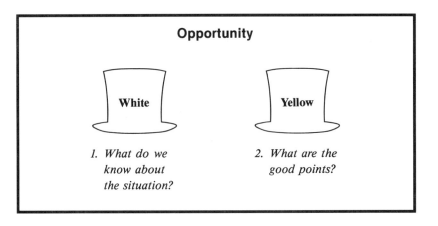

TEACHER NOTES · Sequences

Design

This sequence can be followed for creating new designs. First the blue hat is used to make clear the purpose of the design: needs, constraints, etc. The green hat comes up with some preliminary design ideas or sketches. The red hat then looks at each of these and asks, *Does this feel right?*

Here the red hat thinking is based on intuitions rather than emotions. The designs will need to be checked out with the black hat later, but the first assessment tool for a designer is the red hat.

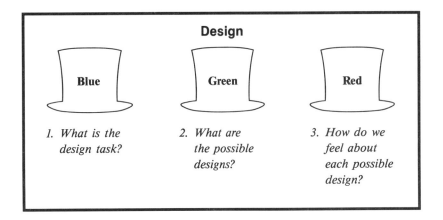

Possibilities

The green hat thinks of all manner of possibilities. Then the blue hat tries to pull together all these possibilities to group them or put them in some order.

This is the basic sequence in an idea-generating session when the background information is known and the ideas are not going to be assessed immediately. The task is to generate the ideas and collect them.

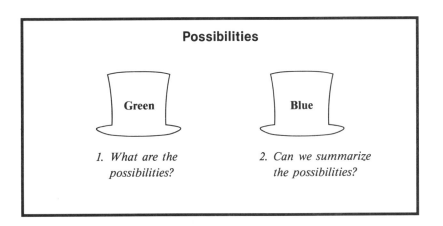

Usable Alternatives

A possibility is only a possibility. In order to turn a possibility into a usable alternative, we need to do some further thinking. We use the yellow hat to strengthen the possibility and to build it up. Then we use the black hat to point out weaknesses.

After noting the weaknesses, we then seek to correct these weaknesses. This could mean the use of the green hat again, but this is not strictly necessary since the use of the black hat in this context is automatically followed by an attempt to put right the weaknesses.

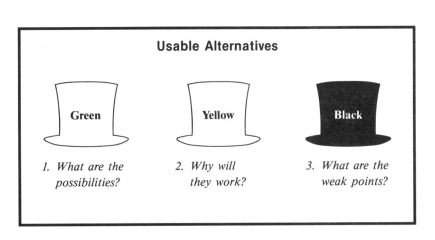

TEACHER NOTES · Sequences

Choice

When we have alternatives, we must choose among them. This sequence is for making choices and decisions. Yellow hat thinking is used to find the good points and also to strengthen the alternatives. Black hat thinking is used to find the weak points so they can be corrected and then to point out the remaining difficulties and dangers.

After yellow and black hat thinking are completed, we have the fully examined alternatives before us. The final choice depends on our feelings, which means the application of our values. If a choice cannot be made, then there is a need to find further alternatives.

Final Assessment

Before any idea is put into action, we must apply the black hat. This way we can avoid mistakes, become aware of potential dangers, and realize the difficulties. Even if the black hat has already been used in choosing an alternative, it is used again in the final assessment. Those who are afraid that the six hats might encourage thinking that is too optimistic should be reassured by this final black hat assessment.

The final black hat is followed by the red hat. Usually if black hat thinking has uncovered many difficulties, red hat thinking will reject the idea. But occasionally we might still like an idea even if it is unworkable or difficult. This means that further thinking will be done to make the idea workable. Or we will take the risk in spite of a full knowledge of the difficulties and dangers.

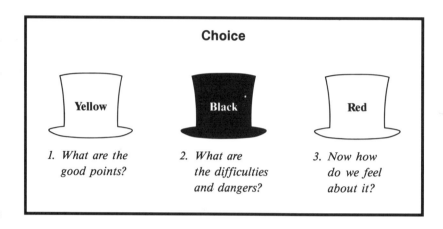

Choice

Yellow — *1. What are the good points?*

Black — *2. What are the difficulties and dangers?*

Red — *3. Now how do we feel about it?*

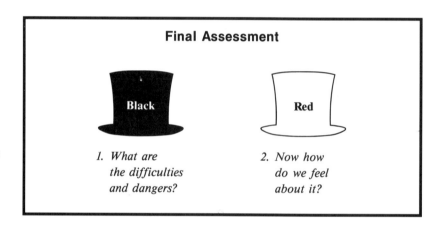

Final Assessment

Black — *1. What are the difficulties and dangers?*

Red — *2. Now how do we feel about it?*

ollow these steps to introduce the sequences: lead-in, explanation, demonstration, practice, and elaboration.

Lead-in

Ask students to imagine that there is a bad storm outside and they are home alone. Their family is not yet home, and the students are getting worried.

Invite students to use the six thinking hats to think about this situation. Suggest that it will take more than one hat to do the job.

> "Let's put on our blue hats. Tell me which hats you would use to think about being home alone in the storm, and why you would choose each hat."

A variety of useful sequences may be offered. Encourage students to explain their suggestions. Comment only if they are confused about the uses of the hats: "The red hat would be for feelings, Jackie. If you want to think of dangers next, you could use the black hat."

Here are a few possible sequences for thinking about the storm.

Sequences

> Green (What are the alternatives?)—Yellow (Why will these work?)—Black (What are the weak points?)

> Red (What do I feel like doing?)—Black (What are the difficulties and dangers?)

> Red (What are my feelings?)—White (What do we already know about the situation?)—Green (What are the alternatives?)—Blue (What is the conclusion?)

To complete the lead-in, make the reproducible **Making a Choice** activity on page 124 available to the students. Read the directions aloud, then give students time to complete the activity. Invite students to share their results with the class. Discussion notes are provided on page 125.

Making a Choice

Edward de Bono / Six Thinking Hats for Schools / 3-5 Resource Book

Directions: An author has written a book in which a clever detective, at great risk to her own safety, stops a plan to secretly bury toxic waste in the desert. Four possible titles for this book have been suggested. Read the titles, then use the hat sequence shown to choose a title. Jot down your thoughts beside each hat.

Titles:

Danger in the Desert

Woman Against Waste

Wanda the Eco-Warrior

The Case of the Disappearing Drums

Yellow _____

Black _____

Red _____

Chosen Title _____

Making a Choice · Discussion Notes

When students have completed the activity, tally the number of votes for each of the four book titles. Then invite students to share their yellow, black, and red hat thinking about the titles. After students have heard each other's thinking, tally the votes again to see if any minds were changed.

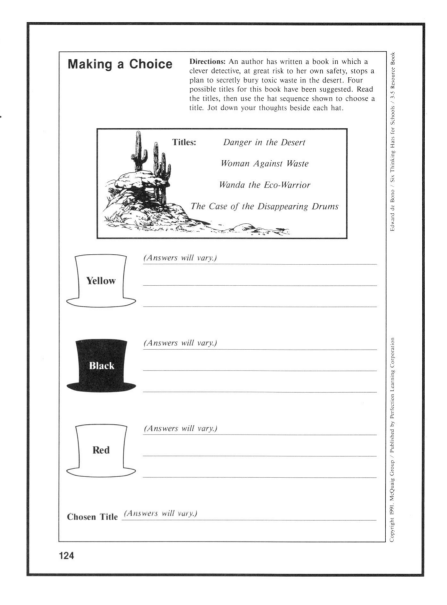

Making a Choice

Directions: An author has written a book in which a clever detective, at great risk to her own safety, stops a plan to secretly bury toxic waste in the desert. Four possible titles for this book have been suggested. Read the titles, then use the hat sequence shown to choose a title. Jot down your thoughts beside each hat.

Titles:
Danger in the Desert

Woman Against Waste

Wanda the Eco-Warrior

The Case of the Disappearing Drums

Yellow *(Answers will vary.)*

Black *(Answers will vary.)*

Red *(Answers will vary.)*

Chosen Title *(Answers will vary.)*

124

Edward de Bono / Six Thinking Hats for Schools / 3-5 Resource Book

Copyright 1991, McQuaig Group / Published by Perfection Learning Corporation

Explanation

After the **Making a Choice** activity has been completed, explain to students that they have just finished using the hats in a *sequence* (in a certain order). Explain that the six thinking hats can be used in many different sequences, some of which will now be discussed.

Give each student a copy of the **Six Thinking Hats Sequences** reproducible chart on pages 127-131. Invite students to outline the hats in color as each sequence is explained. Color coding will make the sequences chart easier to consult at a glance.

As you introduce each sequence, ask one or two of the following questions:

What do you think this sequence would do?

Which of the following things (give choices) would this sequence do?

Why do you think this is the sequence given for (name operation, e.g., choice)?

Describe a time when you might use this sequence.

As an alternative or follow-up, you may wish to help students make flags for some or all of the sequences. Each colored hat can become one vertical band in the flag. For example, the **First Ideas** flag would have a blue band on the left, a white band in the center, and a green band on the right.

The sequence chart and/or flags can make the hats easier to use in your curriculum (see sample applications beginning on page 139).

With younger students or those who find the sequences difficult, you might wish to introduce only a handful of the most useful patterns. In such cases, here is a recommended list:

First Ideas   Direct Action
Evaluation   Opportunity
Improvement   Choice

Six Thinking Hats Sequences

First Ideas

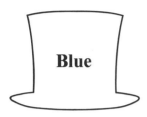 **Blue**

 **White**

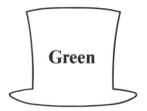 **Green**

1. What is the thinking task?

2. What do we know about the situation?

3. What ideas can we think of?

Quick Assessment

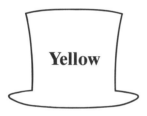 **Yellow**

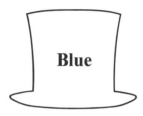 **Blue**

1. What are the good points?

2. Can we summarize the good points?

Evaluation

 **Yellow**

 **Black**

1. What are the good points?

2. What are the difficulties and dangers?

Six Thinking Hats Sequences

Improvement

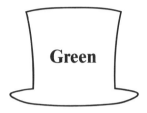

1. What are the weaknesses?

2. How can we overcome them?

Explanation

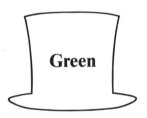

1. What do we know about the situation?

2. What are the possible explanations?

Direct Action

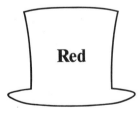

1. What do we feel like doing?

2. What are the difficulties and dangers?

Edward de Bono / Six Thinking Hats for Schools / 3-5 Resource Book

Copyright 1991. McQuaig Group / Published by Perfection Learning Corporation

Six Thinking Hats Sequences

Emotions

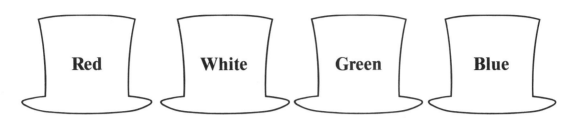

Red	White	Green	Blue

1. How do we feel?   *2. What do we know about the situation?*   *3. What are the alternatives?*   *4. What is the conclusion?*

Caution

White   **Black**

1. What do we know about the situation?   *2. What are the dangers?*

Opportunity

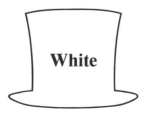 

White   **Yellow**

1. What do we know about the situation?   *2. What are the good points?*

Six Thinking Hats Sequences

Design

Blue

1. What is the design task?

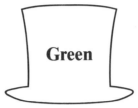

Green

2. What are the possible designs?

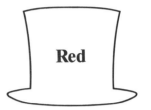

Red

3. How do we feel about each possible design?

Possibilities

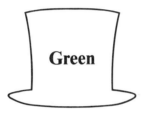

Green

1. What are the possibilities?

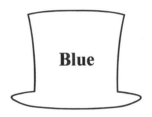

Blue

2. Can we summarize the possibilities?

Usable Alternatives

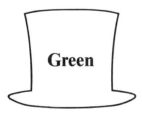

Green

1. What are the possibilities?

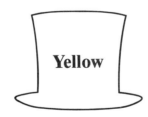

Yellow

2. Why will they work?

Black

3. What are the weak points?

Edward de Bono / Six Thinking Hats for Schools / 3-5 Resource Book

Six Thinking Hats Sequences

Choice

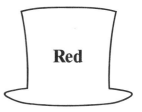

1. What are the good points?

2. What are the difficulties and dangers?

3. Now how do we feel about it?

Final Assessment

1. What are the difficulties and dangers?

2. Now how do we feel about it?

Demonstration

After introducing the sequences, make the **Out in Left Field** reproducible on page 133 available to the students. Read the directions and the narrative aloud, then give students time to write a response. Discussion notes are provided on page 134.

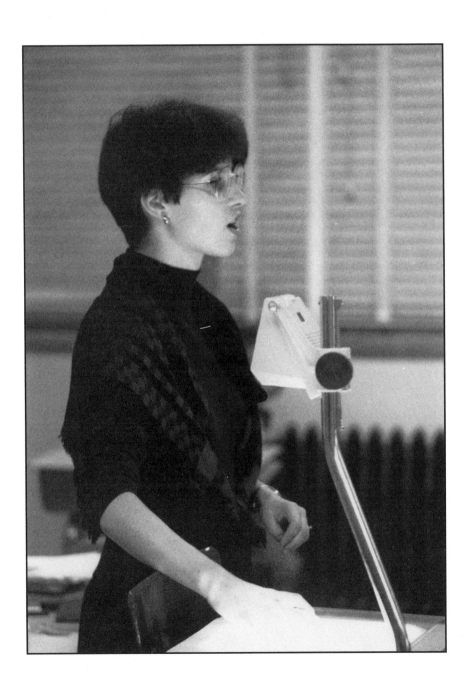

Out in Left Field

Directions: Read about the conflict and then write how the character might think about it using the Emotions Sequence.

Caitlin pitches for the Royals softball team. Lately she has been missing practice, and her pitching hasn't been very good. Still, the coach has kept her first in the batting order, and she is hitting well.

Laura plays left field for the Royals and never misses a practice. But Laura is sixth to bat and often strikes out.

The Royals have lost their last three games. Laura thinks Caitlin's pitching is to blame. She thinks Caitlin should be punished by losing her first batting position.

Since Laura has strong feelings, she has chosen to think about the situation using the Emotions Sequence. Her goal is to decide what action to take.

Beside each hat below, jot down what Laura might think. Since you don't really know her, you are free to invent details.

Emotions Sequence

1. How do I feel?

_____

_____

2. What do I know about the situation?

_____

_____

3. What are the alternatives?

_____

_____

4. What is the conclusion?

_____

_____

Out in Left Field · Discussion Notes

Strong feelings are not right or wrong, but feelings do sometimes need to be put out in the open before any other kind of thinking can take place. You might wish to help students focus on how Laura *does* feel and on what constructive action she can take, rather than debating whether or not she *should* feel that way.

Begin by inviting students to share their writing with a partner. Then ask volunteers to read some of the writings aloud (with the author's permission). Have listeners check to see if the thoughts at each step in the sequence fit the hat. For example, is a given comment really red hat thinking?

Also ask students to notice if the writing shows Laura sticking to her goal: deciding what action to take.

After discussing the activity, invite students to try to apply the Emotions Sequence in their own lives. Encourage them to keep a private record of the results.

A sample conflict resolution activity using the Emotion Sequence appears on page 159 of this book. This activity can be used to apply the six thinking hats when emotional situations arise at school.

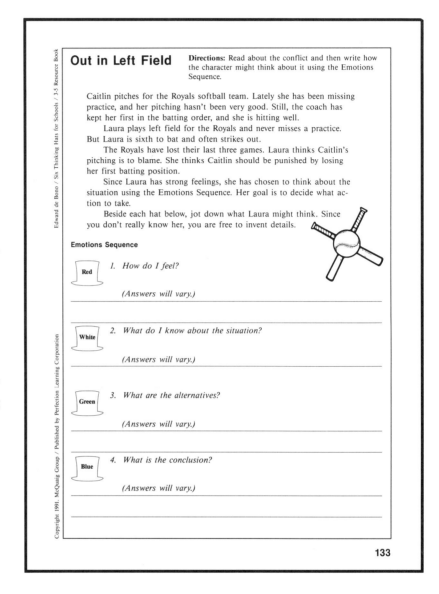

Out in Left Field

Directions: Read about the conflict and then write how the character might think about it using the Emotions Sequence.

Caitlin pitches for the Royals softball team. Lately she has been missing practice, and her pitching hasn't been very good. Still, the coach has kept her first in the batting order, and she is hitting well.

Laura plays left field for the Royals and never misses a practice. But Laura is sixth to bat and often strikes out.

The Royals have lost their last three games. Laura thinks Caitlin's pitching is to blame. She thinks Caitlin should be punished by losing her first batting position.

Since Laura has strong feelings, she has chosen to think about the situation using the Emotions Sequence. Her goal is to decide what action to take.

Beside each hat below, jot down what Laura might think. Since you don't really know her, you are free to invent details.

Emotions Sequence

Red   *1. How do I feel?*

    (Answers will vary.)

White   *2. What do I know about the situation?*

    (Answers will vary.)

Green   *3. What are the alternatives?*

    (Answers will vary.)

Blue   *4. What is the conclusion?*

    (Answers will vary.)

Edward de Bono / Six Thinking Hats for Schools / 3–5 Resource Book

Copyright 1991. McQuaig Group / Published by Perfection Learning Corporation

133

Sequence Practice

The exercises on the next two pages are for the students to tackle on their own. Students may work as individuals or in groups (four or five students). A suggested time is given for each exercise.

Read selected tasks to the students, or reproduce the pages so that each student has a copy. If students have their own copies, you might invite them to select which items they would like to try.

Help students complete the exercises by keeping time for them. After time is up on an exercise, invite students to share their thinking with the group.

Put On Your Six Hats

1. One evening you and a friend walk over to a neighbor's house to shoot baskets. But you find that your neighbor has to stay in and do homework. You and your friend think about what you could do instead. Which of the following sequences would be most useful to you and why?

    First Ideas: blue-white-green

    Explanation: white-green

    Possibilities: green-blue

    Caution: white-black

    Suggested time: 1 minute.

2. A homeroom teacher is trying to choose between two couples to be homeroom parents for her students. Which of the following sequences do you think she should use and why?

    Design: blue-green-red

    Evaluation: yellow-black

    Possibilities: green-blue

    Choice: yellow-black-red

    Suggested time: 1 minute.

3. You need some money to buy something that you want. You have decided that there are four ways to get the money:

    sell something

    borrow the money

    promise to pay for the item later

    do odd jobs to earn the money

    Think about each choice using the Evaluation Sequence (yellow-black). Then use the red hat to make a choice.

    Suggested time: 6 minutes.

Edward de Bono / Six Thinking Hats for Schools / 3-5 Resource Book

Copyright 1991. McQuaig Group / Published by Perfection Learning Corporation

Put On Your Six Hats

4. Someone has written a mean note and put it in your locker. You know who it is and you want to write something mean back. Before doing that, think about the situation using the Direct Action Sequence (red-black).

    Suggested time: 2 minutes.

5. A radio station is giving a free bicycle to the person who designs the best logo for a biker's T-shirt. Choose a sequence and use it to jot down some thoughts about the logo.

    Suggested time: 4 minutes.

6. You have never been to this country before. You step off the plane in a crowded airport. Which of the following simple sequences would be most useful to you and why?

    Caution: white-black

    Final Assessment: black-red

    Opportunity: white-yellow

    Suggested time: 1 minute.

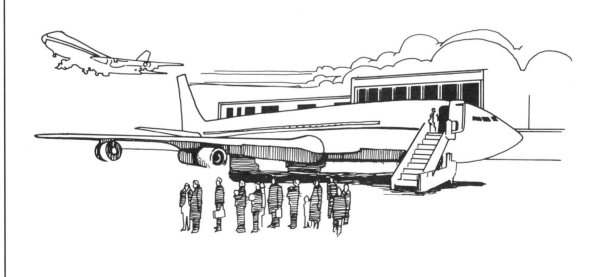

Elaboration

During the practice session, you and your students may have made additional observations on how the six thinking hat sequences are used. After the practice session, invite students to notice the ways they use the sequences in real life and for what purposes.

These observations could be recorded in the students' journals. Invite the class to trade journals, read, and comment on each other's entries.

For further uses of the sequences in the classroom, see pages 139-160.

Conclusion

The six thinking hats can be used in sequences to perform more complicated thinking tasks. The sequences described in this book include the following:

First Ideas: **Blue - White - Green**

Quick Assessment: **Yellow - Blue**

Evaluation: **Yellow - Black**

Improvement: **Black - Green**

Explanation: **White - Green**

Direct Action: **Red - Black**

Emotions: **Red - White - Green - Blue**

Caution: **White - Black**

Opportunity: **White - Yellow**

Design: **Blue - Green - Red**

Possibilities: **Green - Blue**

Usable Alternatives: **Green - Yellow - Black**

Choice: **Yellow - Black - Red**

Final Assessment: **Black - Red**

These fourteen sequences are used in many of the sample applications which follow.

The following model lessons were written by classroom teachers to show some possible ways the six thinking hats can be used across the curriculum. They are offered as springboards for designing your own classroom applications for the six thinking hats.

The models show the hats used in the sequences described in this book and in teacher-created sequences. You are encouraged to use the six thinking hats in any ways that fit the needs of your students and your goals for them.

Sample Application · Language Arts

You're Invited!

Grade: 3

Focus:
Letter writing

Group:
Whole class and small groups

Skills:
Writing, peer review

Materials Needed:
One copy of the **You're Invited! Peer Review** reproducible (see page 141) for each student

Background:
Students should have had some experience writing letters.

Directions:

Prewriting

Green Hat
With your green hat, imagine an event—such as a party, special meal, sports contest, movie, or concert—to which you would like to invite others. Once you have your idea, begin to plan a letter you can write inviting a friend to this event.

Red Hat
Decide the tone of your letter. (*Tone* is the emotion readers feel when reading a work.) Should the invitation be friendly, formal, mysterious, etc.? What red hat feelings do you want readers to have? *(You may wish to give students some examples of writing that establishes a definite tone.)*

White Hat
What white hat facts should you include in your letter? *(You also may wish to ask what white hat facts students know about proper letter form. Supply any missing information they will need.)*

Postwriting

After students have written and revised their letters, ask them to divide into groups of six. Then give each student a copy of the **You're Invited! Peer Review** form on page 141. Ask students to attach the form to their letter and pass their letter to another person in their group.

Encourage student evaluators to respond to the first question on the review sheet and sign their name beside their comments. Then ask them to pass the letter and review sheet to another student. This student responds to the second question. Papers are rotated until the peer review forms are completed. By the end of the rotation, each student will have used each of the six thinking hats once.

You're Invited! Peer Review

1. **White Hat:** What facts does the writer give? What facts, if any, are missing?
   Comments:

   Name:

2. **Red Hat:** What is the tone (feeling) of the letter? Do you think this is the tone the writer wanted the letter to have?
   Comments:

   Name:

3. **Yellow Hat:** What are the good points of the letter?
   Comments:

   Name:

4. **Black Hat:** What are the weaknesses of the letter?
   Comments:

   Name:

5. **Green Hat:** What ideas do you have for improving the letter?
   Comments:

   Name:

6. **Blue Hat:** Summarize the group's thinking about the letter.
   Comments:

   Name:

Sample Application · Language Arts

Teach a Friend an Idiom

Grade: 4

Focus:
Reading comprehension (idioms)

Group:
Whole class and small groups or individuals

Skills:
Understanding literal and figurative meanings, designing

Materials Needed:
One copy of the **Idiom Planner** reproducible (see page 143) for each group or student

Background:
Students should know the definition of idioms and have some experience identifying examples.

Directions:

1. Review the definition of *idiom* with students and give them a few examples. An *idiom* is a saying with a meaning that is different from the usual meanings of the words. Some possibilities are listed below.

   feel under the weather
   act stuck up
   run circles around
   fly by the seat of your pants
   have a green thumb
   cut it out

   Ask students for other examples and write their suggestions on the board.

2. Have students break up into groups. (You may prefer to have students complete this task individually.) Give each group a copy of the **Idiom Planner** reproducible on page 143. Invite students to pick an idiom from the list on the board and to think of several plans for teaching the idiom. Each plan should show the intended (*figurative*) meaning of the idiom and the funny (*literal*) meaning which results when the idiom is read word for word.

Note: If students have problems coming up with ways to teach idioms, generate ideas as a class. Some suggestions: a skit, posters, cartoon strips, stories, pantomimes, greeting cards, bumper stickers, T-shirts, or a collection of quotes (clipped or copied from newspapers, magazines, etc.) showing usage of the idiom.

Follow-up Suggestions:

Have students choose their favorite alternative plan and carry it out. Display their finished work in a classroom Idiom Corner. Or have students test out their designs by showing them to a younger child or a person unfamiliar with the language who may not know the idiom.

FL·ESL·EFL Opportunities:

If you have students who know a foreign language, you might suggest they create a design or plan to teach the meaning of an idiom from that language to the class.

This approach can also be used to teach English idioms to students who are non-English speakers.

Idiom Planner

Date: _____

Name(s): _____

_____

Your Idiom: _____

Review: Idioms have two meanings. One is the intended meaning of the phrase. For example, if we say "It's raining cats and dogs," we intend to say that it is raining very hard. The other meaning is the funny meaning which results if the idiom is taken literally. For example, the funny meaning of "It's raining cats and dogs" is the idea that cats and dogs actually are falling from the sky.

Directions: Use the Usable Alternatives Sequence to think of several plans for teaching your idiom to someone who does not know it. Each plan should show the intended (*figurative*) meaning of the idiom and the funny (*literal*) meaning.

Green Hat: What are some ways to show a person the two meanings of your idiom? Describe, outline, or sketch your favorite ideas.

Yellow Hat: What are the good points about each of your ideas? Why will each one work? List the good points.

Black Hat: What are the weaknesses of each idea? What might confuse people? List the problems.

Green Hat: How can you overcome the problems? Suggest some ways to make each idea better.

After you have thought about each usable alternative, choose the one you like best. Now go ahead and create your lesson.

Sample Application · Language Arts

Inside the Card Catalog

Grade: 5

Focus:
Library skills

Group:
Whole class and small groups or individuals

Skills:
Drawing conclusions, solving problems, summarizing, evaluating, researching

Materials Needed:
An example of an author card, title card, and at least one subject card (presented on poster, blackboard, reproducible, or overhead)

Background:
Students should have visited a library.

Directions:

Explain that the card catalog contains information about every book in the library. Also explain that each book—whether it is fiction or non-fiction—has an author card, title card, and at least one subject card.

Next, show students an example of each card. Make sure all three cards relate to the same book. Then help students think about the card catalog using the Opportunity Sequence.

Opportunity Sequence

White Hat
What information can you see written on the title card? Subject card? Author card? *(Call number, first letter of author's last name, author's full name—last name first— book title, location and name of publisher, year of publication, and sometimes the number of pages, a brief summary, and whether or not there are illustrations.)*

Yellow Hat
What are the benefits of this system? What are the good points about the card catalog cards?

After students have discovered some opportunities offered by the card catalog, ask them to think about the following situation using the Possibilities Sequence.

Imagine that you are writing a paper about how whales and dolphins are alike and how they are different. Think about this task using the Possibilities Sequence.

Possibilities Sequence

Green Hat
How might you find resources for this paper using the card catalog?

Blue Hat
Summarize your ideas.

Follow-up Suggestion:

Have students pick a topic of their own. Then ask them to check the card catalog for some resources they could consult for information about their topic. This activity could be done in small groups or by individuals.

Sample Application · Social Studies

On the Move

Grade: 3

Focus:
World studies, geography

Group:
Small groups, partners, or individuals

Skills:
Summarizing, comparing and contrasting, predicting, analyzing

Directions:

Following a survey of the characteristics of a particular state, country, or area, invite students to meet in small groups to summarize knowledge and exchange ideas about the area. Then have students use their knowledge to think about the following proposal.

> Suppose your family is moving to _____ [area of study] in one month. Think about this move using the six hats Emotions and Evaluation sequences.

Emotions Sequence

Red Hat
How do you feel about the move? What are your red hat ideas?

White Hat
What are some important facts about the place where you will live? List white hat ideas.

Green Hat
What different experiences will you find or can you create in your new home? Give your green hat ideas.

Blue Hat
What will you do when you arrive in your new home? Draw a blue hat conclusion from all your thinking.

Evaluation Sequence

Yellow Hat
What might be the good points of your plan of action? List your yellow hat ideas.

Black Hat
What might be the problems or weaknesses in your plan? Give your black hat thoughts.

Sample Application · Social Studies

Pieces of the Past

Grade: 4

Focus:
World culture, archaeology

Group:
Small groups

Skills:
Explaining, hypothesizing, drawing conclusions, analyzing

Materials Needed:
Pictures of objects from ancient cultures or actual objects (Make sure nothing on the picture or object states what it is. However, for ease of discussion and identification, number each artifact.)

One copy of the **Pieces of the Past** reproducible (see page 147) for each group

Background:
Students should have been exposed to the history of other cultures and should know what artifacts are.

Directions:

Review with students the meaning of *artifact.* Also help them define what an archaeologist is and does.

Then have students divide up into "archaeology teams." Give each group an "artifact"—a picture or object to study.

Also hand out the reproducible **Pieces of the Past** (page 147). The questions on that reproducible will help students examine some possible explanations for the artifacts.

Follow-up Suggestions:

You may wish to have each group present their findings and conclusions before the class and then invite class response. Or you could have each group write a report and post the paper, along with the artifacts, in a cross-cultural display.

Pieces of the Past

Date: _____

Artifact number: _____

Group members: _____

White Hat
What facts do you know about the artifact? List them.

Green Hat
What might your artifact be? List some possibilities.

Yellow Hat
What are the good points about each of your possible explanations?
Why might each one be correct? List the good points below.

Black Hat
What are the weaknesses of each possible explanation? Why might each
one be incorrect? List the problems below.

Green Hat
How can you overcome the problems? Suggest some ways to make the
case for each possible explanation stronger.

Red Hat
Now that you have thought about the possibilities, which explanation
do you like best?

Sample Application · Social Studies

Westward Ho!

Grade: 5

Focus:
United States history

Group:
Whole class and small groups or individuals

Skills:
Summarizing, researching, solving problems, evaluating, predicting

Materials Needed:
Research material on the history of a United States area chosen by you or students

Background:
Students should have some familiarity with the history of the United States and the pioneer migrations to the West.

Directions:

Remind students that pioneers traveled west by foot, horseback, or wagon. Therefore, they had room for only the basics and a few prized items. There were few trading posts or stores along the way. So pioneers had to be sure to take supplies they needed to survive.

Have students imagine they are pioneers in the _____ and that they are going to migrate west to _____. (You or students supply time period and area in the United States.) Their wagon is waiting, and it's time to load their chosen supplies.

Invite students to decide what they will take with them by using the First Ideas and Choice sequences.

First Ideas Sequence

Blue Hat
Put on your blue hat and redefine the thinking task. What are you supposed to think about?

White Hat
What white hat facts and information do you have? *(Students may need a chance to do some research at this point.)*

Green Hat
Use the green hat to think of some things you want to take with you. What suggestions can you come up with?

Now pick six items that are essential to take with you. Then complete the following sequence to explore your choices.

Choice Sequence

Yellow Hat
What are the good points about your choices? List your yellow hat ideas.

Black Hat
What problems might you face because of your choices? Give your black hat thoughts.

Red Hat
Use your red hat to tell how you feel about your choices.

Sample Application · Science

Saving the Environment

Grade: 3

Focus:
Ecology

Group:
Whole class

Skills:
Observing, drawing conclusions, classifying, analyzing, making decisions

Background:
Prior to completing the following activity, the students should be able to identify those practices of institutions and individuals that are harmful to the environment, tell why those practices are harmful, and suggest ways of changing behaviors and purchasing patterns to make them more environmentally sound.

Directions:

This activity would most logically be included at the end of a unit on natural resources or environmental awareness, or as a prelude to the celebration of Earth Day. The purpose of the activity is to use several thinking hat sequences to devise and implement a plan for a small step toward saving the Earth.

First Ideas Sequence

Blue Hat
Help students define the purpose of the thinking session: to plan a safe environment project which will help reduce environmental damage. Suggest that they might use the First Ideas and the Choice sequences to structure their thinking.

White Hat
Have students list practices in their school that are environmentally unsafe. Then ask them which of those listed items they can control or influence.

Green Hat
Invite students to suggest ways they could do something about the items on the list to improve their school environment.

Choice Sequence

Yellow Hat
What are the good points about each of your ideas for improving your school environment? Why will each one work?

Black Hat
What are the weaknesses of each idea? What is wrong with each? List the problems below.

Red Hat
Which of your ideas do you like best?

Follow-up Suggestion:

Implement the chosen ideas over a period of time. Then assess the effectiveness of the plan using the Evaluation Sequence. Help the class decide whether to continue with the improvement plan, adopt another safe practice, try to implement their plan on a school- or district-wide basis, or end the experiment.

Sample Application · Science

Linked for Life

Grades: 4-5

Focus:
Food chain

Group:
Whole class or small groups

Skills:
Researching, summarizing, hypothesizing, evaluating

Materials Needed:
Resource materials on mice

Background:
Students should have knowledge of the food chain and the delicate balance that exists in nature.

Directions:

Review the concept of the food chain. Then ask students to think about what would happen if the mouse disappeared from the food chain. Allow students some time to think about the question and do some research about mice. Then have them use the Explanation and Evaluation sequences to process the information they have gathered.

Explanation Sequence

White Hat
What are some important facts about the mouse and its place in the food chain? List some white hat facts.

Green Hat
What might happen if the mouse disappeared? Give some green hat ideas.

Evaluation Sequence

Yellow Hat
What are the good points about the disappearance of the mouse from the food chain? Give your yellow hat thinking.

Black Hat
What are the bad points about the disappearance of the mouse from the food chain? Give your black hat thinking.

Sample Application · Math

Addition or Multiplication?

Grade: 3

Focus:
Addition, multiplication

Group:
Whole class

Skills:
Comparing and contrasting, adding, multiplying

Materials Needed:
Overhead projector and transparencies with problems similar to the following:

```
  3        3        2        2
  3      × 5        2      × 7
  3       ---       2       ---
  3        15       2        14
  3                 2
+ 3                 2
 ---                2
  15              + 2
                   ---
                    14
```

Background:
Students should have been introduced to the concept of multiplication and should have studied problems up to and including the 5s. At this point, memorization of the multiplication tables becomes increasingly necessary, and this may meet with resistance. This thinking exercise should help define the benefits of using multiplication in order to perform more rapid computation.

Directions:
Put the transparency up on the screen. Work through some simple addition and corresponding multiplication problems with the class. Then ask students the following thinking hat questions.

Choice Sequence

Yellow Hat
Put on your yellow hats. What are the good points about working the problems using addition skills? What are the good points about working the problems using multiplication skills?

Black Hat
Now put on your black hats. What are the difficulties in working the problems using addition skills? What are the difficulties in working the problems using multiplication skills?

Red Hat
Finally, what are your red hat ideas? How do you feel now about the concept of addition? the concept of multiplication?

Sample Application · Math

Measure for Measure

Grade: 4

Focus:
Measurement

Group:
Small groups or individuals

Skills:
Solving problems, analyzing, evaluating

Background:
This activity may be used before or after students have learned about measurement.

Directions:

Have students imagine themselves in the following situation. Then ask them to think of solutions by using the Usable Alternatives Sequence.

Your boat has crashed and you are left alone on a desert island. To be more comfortable, you would like to build a hut. You have most of the tools to do this since you saved a tool box from your sunken boat. However, there is no tape measure or ruler in the tool box. How can you measure things?

Usable Alternatives Sequence

Green Hat
How can you measure building materials such as tree limbs, rocks, leaves, or vines for constructing your hut? Put on your green hat and list some possible ways.

Yellow Hat
What are the good points about each of your ideas? Why will each one work? List the good points.

Black Hat
What are the weaknesses of each idea? What is wrong with each? List the problems.

Green Hat
Think of some ways to correct those problems. What green hat suggestions can you come up with?

Follow-up Suggestion:

Divide the class into groups and have them use their green hat ideas to build cardboard huts. Encourage students to modify their measurement techniques during the process if they discover better ways. At the end of the project, ask students to use the Evaluation Sequence to decide how effective their measurement techniques were.

Sample Application · Math

Spotting Number Patterns

Grade: 5

Focus:
Number patterns

Group:
Whole class and small groups

Skills:
Adding, dividing, drawing conclusions, identifying patterns

Materials Needed:
A copy of the **Spotting Number Patterns** reproducible (see page 154) for each student

Background:
Students should know how to add, subtract, multiply, and divide.

Directions:

Give each student a **Spotting Number Patterns** chart (see page 154). Explain that number patterns are hidden within the chart.

Teacher-Created Sequence

White Hat
Let's do some white hat thinking.

1. Circle the first row of numbers from 0-9. Then look at the numbers carefully. Go across the row from 0 to 9 and double each number. So A + A = 2A.

   When you finish, compare your sums—2A to 2B, 2B to 2C, etc. What pattern can you see?

   (When you double a number, its total will be 2 less than the double of the next consecutive number. So 2A = 2B − 2 or 2A + 2 = 2B.)

2. Circle any three consecutive numbers going across, like 32, 33, 34 or 74, 75, 76. Add those three numbers together. Then take the answer and divide it by three—which is how many numbers you circled. Do this with another two sets of three numbers.

   Look at the answers. What pattern can you see?

   (The final answer is always the middle number of the original three. So 74 + 75 + 76 = 225 and 225 ÷ 3 = 75.)

3. Now try adding five consecutive numbers together. Then divide by five. Try this with several different sets of five consecutive numbers. What pattern can you see?

   (The final answer is always the middle number of the first five.)

Green Hat
Get in your groups and put on your green hats. See how many other patterns you can locate in the 0-99 number chart.

Blue Hat
Share your patterns with the class. Put on your blue hat and summarize what you found.

Spotting Number Patterns

Directions:

White Hat

1. Circle the first row of numbers from 0-9. Then look at the numbers carefully. Go across the row from 0 to 9 and double each number. (For example, A + A = 2A.) When you finish, compare your sums. What pattern can you see?

2. Circle any three consecutive numbers going across, like 32, 33, 34 or 74, 75, 76. Add those three numbers together. Then take the answer and divide it by three—which is how many numbers you circled. Do this with another two sets of three numbers. Look at the answers. What pattern can you see?

3. Add five consecutive numbers together. Then divide by five. Try this with several different sets of five consecutive numbers. What pattern can you see?

Green Hat

See how many other patterns you can locate in the 0-99 number chart.

0	1	2	3	4	5	6	7	8	9
10	11	12	13	14	15	16	17	18	19
20	21	22	23	24	25	26	27	28	29
30	31	32	33	34	35	36	37	38	39
40	41	42	43	44	45	46	47	48	49
50	51	52	53	54	55	56	57	58	59
60	61	62	63	64	65	66	67	68	69
70	71	72	73	74	75	76	77	78	79
80	81	82	83	84	85	86	87	88	89
90	91	92	93	94	95	96	97	98	99

Edward de Bono / Six Thinking Hats for Schools / 3-5 Resource Book

Sample Application - Art

Making a Mural

Grades: 3-4

Focus:
Mixed media illustration

Group:
Small groups

Skills:
Planning, designing, creating

Materials Needed:
Long sheet of butcher paper or some other background surface, paints and brushes, chalk or crayons, scraps of paper or cloth, scissors, glue

Directions:

Discuss what murals are and how they are made. Show students some examples of murals if possible. Help students decide on a subject or theme for a mural that they will create as a group. This might be an underwater scene, map of the neighborhood, scene from a book they are reading, or fantasy world, for example. Then invite them to use the First Ideas Sequence to plan their work.

First Ideas Sequence

Blue Hat
What is your task? What do you need to think about to plan the task?

White Hat
What equipment and materials do you need to make a mural? How long will it take to make the mural?

Green Hat
What are some ideas for creating the images for the mural? How can you carry out those ideas?

Now have students break into groups to complete segments of the mural. Ask one group to paint the background while others make the specific details such as buildings, people, plants, clouds, and so on. Then invite students to attach their individual contributions to the mural.

Once students finish, suggest they use the Evaluation Sequence to discuss any final improvements or changes.

Evaluation Sequence

Yellow Hat
What are the good things about your mural?

Black Hat
What is wrong with the mural? What are the weaknesses?

Red Hat
How do you feel about your mural?

Sample Application · Art

African Masks

Grade: 5

Focus:
Three-dimensional forms

Group:
Whole class

Skills:
Comparing and contrasting, drawing conclusions, designing, executing a design

Materials Needed:
Books on African or primitive art, wood or clay for carving, papier-mâché supplies, cardboard, paper, glue, scissors, paints and brushes, miscellaneous materials for ornamentation (small beads, feathers, bits of leather)

Background:
If possible, a trip to an art museum featuring an exhibit of African masks would be an excellent prelude to this activity. Books or films discussing tribal customs and mythology would also give students a feel for the history and purpose of the masks as they are actually used.

Directions:
Invite students to design and create an African mask by using the First Ideas and Improvement sequences.

First Ideas Sequence

Blue Hat
Outline the goals and procedure to be used to complete this project. Suggest that white hat thinking be used to gather information about styles of masks. Then suggest that students use their green hats to create their own masks. Also encourage them to use the Improvement Sequence to add finishing touches to the project.

White Hat
Using the art books (see Materials Needed) and information gathered from field trips or films, collect data on African masks. What materials and designs are used? What kind of ornamentation is displayed? What sizes and shapes do you see in the masks? What colors are used?

Green Hat
Ask students to use the information they have collected and their imaginations to generate a design for their own African mask. During this time, students also may use white hat thinking as they consider time and materials available for completing their projects.

Improvement Sequence

Black Hat
What are the weaknesses in your mask design? What is wrong with it?

Green Hat
How can you overcome these weaknesses? What can you do to improve your mask?

Red Hat
How do you feel about your finished product?

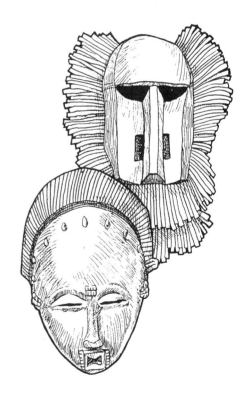

Sample Application · Music

American Indian Dancing

Grade: 3

Focus:
Dance

Group:
Whole class

Skills:
Drawing conclusions, coordinating movements to music, creating

Materials Needed:
Recordings of American Indian dance music, story and dance instructions for at least one of the songs, record or cassette player

Background:
Students should have studied American Indian customs and mythology.

Directions:

Invite students to learn and perform a dance set to American Indian music by using a teacher-created sequence.

Teacher-Created Sequence

Red Hat
Play a recording of several selections of American Indian music for students. After each song, stop and ask the students what mood they sensed in the music. How did the music make them feel?

White Hat
Replay the one song for which the students will be learning the dance. Provide them with background information regarding the tribal origins of the music and the story being told by the song. Teach them the steps to the dance and provide time for practice and rehearsal.

Green Hat
Encourage students to give a final performance of the song. This might be for peers, parents, or just for fun in class. Remind students to listen to the music and to remember the steps they learned. Invite them to add their own touches to the performance, including costumes, facial expressions, or hand flourishes. Students may also enjoy creating an entirely original dance for a different song.

Sample Application · Music

Selecting a Musical Instrument

Grades: 4 and up

Focus:
Instrumental

Group:
Whole class, small groups, or individuals

Skills:
Analyzing, making predictions, comparing and contrasting, drawing conclusions

Materials Needed:
At least one example of each of those instruments taught in the instrumental band program of your school

Background:
This procedure was designed to help prospective band students choose the instrument they would like to play. Students should already be familiar with the names of the instruments and the school's instrumental program. Because parental support is necessary for success in this case, it may be wise to include parents in the process.

Directions:
Invite students to think about the process of choosing a musical instrument to play. Remind them that is an important decision because it is accompanied by a personal investment of time, talent, and often money. Suggest that they use the thinking hats to help them make such a decision wisely: white to gather factual information, yellow to think of good points or benefits, black to identify difficulties, and then red to measure personal preferences. These last three hats compose the Choice Sequence.

White Hat
Provide a basic introduction to each instrument, including the sound it makes, how it works, ease of playing, maintenance, cost if purchased, and so forth. Students should be given the opportunity to ask other white hat questions they may have, and they may want to record this information to review later.

Choice Sequence

Yellow Hat
For each instrument, students ask themselves, "What are the good points?" What would be the benefits of playing this instrument?

Black Hat
For each instrument, students identify black hat points. What would be the bad points about playing this instrument?

Red Hat
Students are now ready to make a choice. How do they feel? Which instrument do they want to play?

Sample Application · Conflict Resolution

Conflict Resolution

Grades: 3 and up

Focus:
Human relations, social skills

Group:
2 individuals with a conflict
1 peer mediator (optional)

Skills:
Expressing feelings, seeing other points of view, distinguishing fact from opinion, considering alternatives

Background:
Students should be familiar with six thinking hats and the kind of thinking each hat stands for. This procedure can be used along with peer mediation programs. In this case, the mediator would be responsible for much of the blue hat thinking, specifically making sure the Emotions Sequence is being followed and that conflicting students keep on track as they search for a resolution.

Emotions Sequence

Red Hat
Use this hat to vent emotions that may prevent clear thinking. If you are dealing with a problem that has just arisen, chances are that feelings are obvious. However, some problems take days or weeks to surface, or resolving a problem must wait until after class or school is dismissed. In such cases, the conflicting parties may want to restate their feelings about the situation. Individuals should be allowed to express their emotions, such as anger, sadness, or confusion.

White Hat
Ask each student to identify what is known about the situation—the facts relevant to the problem. A mediator can help elicit this information.

Green Hat
Once the problem has been identified, encourage each student to think of possible solutions to the conflict. A mediator can assist with this as well.

Blue Hat
At this point, it is possible that a mutually agreeable resolution has been created. If this is not the case, all possible solutions should be assessed using the Evaluation Sequence of yellow-black hat thinking. Then use the blue hat again to draw a conclusion.

Sample Application · Conflict Avoidance

Conflict Avoidance

Grades: 3-5

Focus:
Human relations, social skills

Group:
1 student, a pair, or a group

Skills:
Predicting consequences, considering alternatives, making decisions

Background:
Students should be familiar with six thinking hats and the kind of thinking each hat represents.

Directions:

The following procedures can be introduced to a group of students, but they are designed to be used by individuals. The two sequences need not be used at the same time. The circumstances of given situations will dictate when each should be considered.

A student's use of these sequences can be prompted by a teacher or peer, but they will be most effectively used when the student automatically employs these strategies. In either case, the student will be making a more conscious decision about his or her involvement in conflict situations.

Caution Sequence

White Hat
Before becoming involved in an interaction with peers, a student first reviews the relevant facts. For example, a student may approach a group of students known to cause problems or with whom he or she is incompatible. Or the student may be asked to join in an activity that violates school policy or in some way endangers the health and safety of others.

Black Hat
After defining the nature of the situation, the student considers the possible dangers accompanying personal involvement. This is a quick, informal mental overview.

Direct Action Sequence

Red Hat
The student has an emotional response to a situation, either in the classroom or elsewhere in the school. For instance, the student may feel angry, embarrassed, or frightened. An immediate impulse is to act on the emotion, which may result in conflict with a peer or faculty member.

Black Hat
Before taking the action, the student does some black hat thinking on the possible consequences. This is a quick, informal review of the difficulties and dangers existing in the situation at hand and a prediction of additional dangers that would exist as a result of the action the student may take.

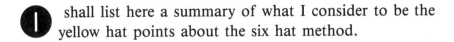

I shall list here a summary of what I consider to be the yellow hat points about the six hat method.

1. The method provides a colorful and fun way of paying attention to thinking. Thinking is usually abstract and boring.

2. The colors and the hats provide a useful mental image that is easy to learn and easy to remember.

3. The six hat method may be used at the simplest possible level but may also be used at a sophisticated level. It has already been in use with six-year-olds and with senior executives in the world's largest businesses.

4. The hats provide a framework for organizing thinking so that it is no longer a matter of drift and argument. Thinking becomes more focused, more constructive, and more productive.

5. In a family, community, school, or organization, once the hats have been learned they become a sort of language for discussing thinking.

6. The hats avoid confusion by allowing a thinker to do just one thing at a time and to do that well.

7. The hats provide a thinking step to do next. They can also provide an overall agenda or framework to guide thinking.

8. The hats can be used to request a certain type of thinking or to request a change from a type of thinking. Taken together this can mean a request for a *switch* in thinking.

9. Because of their artificiality, the hats can be used to ask for a change in thinking without giving offense.

10. The game and role-playing nature of the hats allows for the detachment of the ego from the thinking: "This is not me, but my red hat thinking." This is most important for good thinking.

11. The hats acknowledge that emotions, feelings, and intuition are an important part of practical thinking. The hats allow feelings to come into thinking at the most useful time instead of coming in at the most destructive time.

12. The hats allow full attention to be paid to the critical aspects of thinking (black hat), the constructive aspects of thinking (yellow hat), and the creative aspects of thinking (green hat). Thinking is too often just critical in nature. The hats show that critical thinking is an important part of thinking—but is just one part.

13. The six hat method is easy to teach and easy to learn.

14. The hats provide a framework for learning about the different aspects of thinking and for understanding thinking. Without them, it can be difficult to teach thinking.

15. The hats provide a method for teaching different habits and operations in thinking. These find their place under the different hats. For example, the habits of critical thinking fit naturally under the black hat.

16. Important aspects of thinking, such as formulating hypotheses, speculating, and identifying possibilities, can be taught in a practical manner (green hat).

17. The blue hat provides a simple way of doing the most difficult thing—thinking about thinking. The ability to stand back and watch and control one's own thinking is essential for good thinking but very difficult to teach. The blue hat makes this metacognition more accessible.

18. The six hats provide a simple and practical method for spreading good thinking habits since the hats can easily be explained to other people.

19. The six hats are so basic that they cut across boundaries of culture and ideology. All hats are important. All hats are of great value.

20. The hats provide a simple and practical way of showing that thinking is a skill that can be learned, practiced, and improved. The hats show that thinking is not just a matter of intelligence, of information, or of arguing.

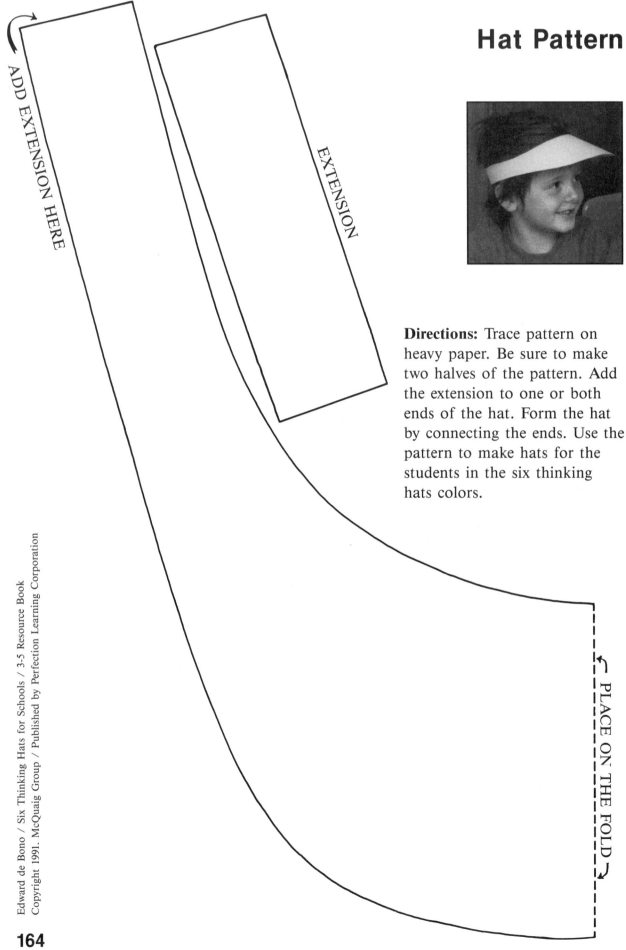

Hat Pattern

ADD EXTENSION HERE

EXTENSION

PLACE ON THE FOLD

Directions: Trace pattern on heavy paper. Be sure to make two halves of the pattern. Add the extension to one or both ends of the hat. Form the hat by connecting the ends. Use the pattern to make hats for the students in the six thinking hats colors.

Hat Pattern

Edward de Bono / Six Thinking Hats for Schools / 3-5 Resource Book
Copyright 1991. McQuaig Group / Published by Perfection Learning Corporation

Edward de Bono Thinking Skills Programs Published by Perfection Learning

Six Thinking Hats for Schools
Teacher Resource Books
    Grades K-2
    Grades 3-5
    Grades 6-8
    Grades 9-12
    Adult Educators
Six Thinking Hats Wall Chart
Six Thinking Hats Journal
Six Thinking Hats Board Game

Think, Note, Write Student
Workbooks and Teacher Guides
    Green Level (Grade 6), Books 1 and 2
    Blue Level (Grade 7), Books 1 and 2
    Red Level (Grade 8), Books 1 and 2
    Purple Level (Grade 9), Books 1 and 2
Think, Note, Write Reproducible Tool Boxes
Think, Note, Write Posters (set of 18)